Martin Walker was born in Darlington, County Durham and attended schools in Durham and London. He won a Brackenbury Scholarship to Balliol College, Oxford and gained a first class degree in Modern History. He was awarded a Commonwealth Fellowship to the US and was a resident tutor at Kirkland House, Harvard, where he studied International Relations. He was a Fellow of the American Political Science Association at the US Congress and a foreign policy aide and speech writer to Senator Ed Muskie when he was running for the presidency against Nixon.

He then joined the *Guardian* as a reporter, columnist, foreign correspondent and features writer. In 1984 he moved to Moscow as the *Guardian*'s first resident correspondent for fifty years.

He has written three non-fiction books, *The National Front*, *Powers of the Press* and *The Waking Giant* and three novels, *An Eastern Question*, *A Mercenary Calling* and *The Infiltrator*.

He is a qualified pilot and is married with two daughters.

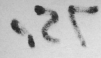

Also by Martin Walker in Abucus:
THE WAKING GIANT

MARTIN WALKER'S RUSSIA:

Despatches from the Guardian correspondent in Moscow

Martin Walker

SPHERE BOOKS

Published by the Penguin Group
27 Wrights Lane, London W8 5TZ, England
Viking Penguin Inc., 40 West 23rd Street, New York, New York 10010, USA
Penguin Books Australia Ltd, Ringwood, Victoria, Australia
Penguin Books Canada Ltd, 2801 John Street, Markham, Ontario, Canada L3R 1B4
Penguin Books (NZ) Ltd, 182–190 Wairau Road, Auckland 10, New Zealand

Penguin Books Ltd, Registered Offices: Harmondsworth, Middlesex, England

These articles were first published in Great Britain by
the *Guardian* as a weekly column.
This collected edition first published in Great Britain
in Abacus by Sphere Books Ltd, 1989
Copyright in this edition © by Martin Walker, 1989

1 3 5 7 9 10 8 6 4 2

Printed and bound in Great Britain by
Richard Clay Ltd, Bungay, Suffolk

03743731

46572075 7
5.6.89

For Kate and Fanny

Contents

Introduction

It is all the fault of Mikhail Gorbachev. If he had not come to power in March of 1985 and launched his astonishing package of reform and controlled revolution upon the Soviet Union, then he would not have caught the imagination of the Western world. There would have been little interest or audience for a book, or a style of journalism such as this.

Indeed, the *Guardian* column 'Martin Walker's Russia' was a child of glasnost. It first began to appear in the late spring of 1986, the month after Chernobyl, when the long traditions of pathological secrecy began to give way to Gorbachev's policy of telling the Soviet people very much more of the truth. But the roots of the column went back rather further. When the *Guardian* opened its Moscow bureau in 1984, we did so hoping that we could break away from some of the clichés and inhibitions which had made us unhappy with most Western reporting about the Soviet Union. My colleagues and editors, Peter Preston, and Richard Gott and Martin Woollacott, urged me to try and write about the place as if it were just another country, rather than Ronald Reagan's 'evil empire'.

My only qualification to write about the place was the fresh eye that comes from ignorance. I was still learning Russian, and could hardly read *Pravda*, let alone the Kremlin's entrails. The arcane and black arts of the professional Sovietologist were beyond me. They were also, in those last stagnant months before the Gorbachev revolution, rather boring. It was much more interesting to find out how people lived, how Russians got their flats, where and how they obtained their food, and how they enjoyed themselves. And it quickly became plain, from the letters we began to receive from *Guardian* readers, that these were the kinds of things they too wanted to know about the Soviet Union. Only a handful of experts in Britain were much concerned about the pecking order of the lower reaches of the Politburo. But women everywhere were appalled to learn that the world's second most powerful state, a pioneer of space travel, produced neither sanitary towels nor tampons for its female citizens.

The luck of the *Guardian* saw to it that we arrived in Moscow in time to catch an entire society of 280 million people poised for transformation. The place was pregnant with change even before Gorbachev took power. It was clear in the frustration of the Soviet officials I began to meet, in the suppressed creativities of the rock music and cultural underground, in the healthy energies of the black and grey markets.

And glasnost began to mean that it was much easier for a Western journalist to function in Moscow, as regular press conferences and briefings steadily accustomed a suspicious bureaucracy to our presence and our questions. Then the Soviet media began to ask me and other Western colleagues to write for their papers, and give interviews and talks on Soviet radio and TV. There was no censorship, even when I wrote an article saying it was time to build a public monument to the victims of Stalin's purges. When I had first arrived in Moscow, they never talked about the purges. The acceptable euphemism was 'the cult of personality', which makes it sound as if the old brute was guilty of a breach of table manners.

So this book is a kind of weekly diary of glasnost and perestroika and the Gorbachev revolution. Or at least, of its thrilling early years. We still do not know if the country will succeed in hauling itself out of the straitjacket, whether a country so vast and so set in its ways and so accustomed to authoritarian rule from the top can be changed – by consent. We do not know if Gorbachev is right in his conviction that socialism and democracy and the Communist Party's monopoly of power can all co-exist. We can only wish him luck, and applaud his desire to make the world a less dangerous place. At the same time, before actually turning all the swords into ploughshares it is worth bearing in mind that Gorbachev's successor might not be so keen to stop the arms race.

I must thank the editor of the *Guardian* for publishing my column on Monday mornings, and encouraging me to recycle many of the articles here. Mr Gennady Gerasimov, head of the information department of the Soviet foreign ministry, and the Kremlin spokesman, helped make my job, and that of a whole generation of Western journalists, very much easier. Many colleagues in the Soviet and Western press gave me assistance, ideas and their friendship. It will be clear from the articles that they could not have been written without the inspiration and support and hospitality of a great many Soviet friends and guides and contacts. Above all, Nina Nikolaevna, my colleague, guide and secretary in the *Guardian*'s Moscow bureau, is virtually the co-author of this book. She had most of the good ideas for it, and talked me out of most of the bad ones. The book is dedicated to my daughters, Kate and Fanny, who make guest appearances in various stories, in the hope that the place will continue to become more fun, more friendly, more free, and yet remain as fascinating.

Martin Walker, Moscow, 1988

1
Wheeling and Dealing

A black market is Nature's way of telling a government to stop interfering. Since the Soviet government interferes more than most, its citizens wheel and deal and barter and borrow and generally acquire virtually everything that is not nailed down, and much that is. With the possible exception of West Africa and the cocaine economy of Bolivia, it is the most corrupt society I have ever known.

The corruption is so widespread that it has a cheerful innocence about it. Everybody knows where the black markets are to be found, and how many roubles there are to the dollar. The state says two roubles are worth three dollars. The street says one dollar is worth three roubles. There is even a good Russian verb, 'derzhat', for being lucky or skilful enough to get hold of something. There is another word for the vital commodity that is usually required. It is 'blat', and it can be translated as influence or pull. For example, when I wanted to spend a weekend at the excellent Riga art festival, the only hotel available to foreigners said it was full. So I rang a Minister in the Latvian government to say how sorry I was that I would not be able to interview him and write my article about his local art festival. Within ten minutes, the hotel suddenly found some spare rooms. This is 'blat'. For Russians, it is a far more important and delicate business. In general terms, the blat of your boss at work, be it a factory or an academic institute, can be measured by the quality of food available at the works canteen. In personal terms, you will need blat to get your child into one of the special schools for foreign languages, or into Moscow University or MGIMO, the institute which trains the Soviet diplomatic corps. Blat could delay your son's conscription to the Army, or ensure that he was not sent to Afghanistan. Blat, or straightforward bribery, can get you into a special hospital when you are ill, and obtain rare imported drugs to make you better.

Blat is neither straightforward crime, nor free enterprise, but occupies a kind of twilight zone between the two. But these categories tend to spill over into one another. Most crime is economic in motive, and the state's traditional dislike of private enterprise has left this sector, including the peasants' markets, vulnerable to Mafia-style extortion and organized crime.

The Soviet Union is a society where almost nothing is legal, but everything is possible. This chapter explains how.

Cold comfit farm
5 March 1985

Although the snow along Serpukhovsky Boulevard still lies deep enough to cover the seats of the park benches, this has been the first official weekend of spring in Russia. Along the main streets of Moscow, the kiosks that normally sell ice cream and hot doughnuts have been selling special springtime cake of crescent-shaped shortbread and hot pastries.

On the balconies of the tower blocks, workmen use long poles to knock off the deadly icicles, three and four feet long, that have hung poised over the pavements all winter. On top of the deep packed snow of the courtyards, there is a grudging inch or so of grey slush.

Just as the old Catholic missionaries of the Dark Ages carefully timed all the Christian festivals to merge with and supplant the pagan celebrations of mid-winter and the spring and autumn equinoxes, so the Soviet state has developed its own alternatives to Easter and Christmas.

By accident, because we had run out of butter, we came across one of the mechanisms of celebration at the weekend. Sunday is a day of rest in Russia, but the official figures suggest that about one person in three is supposed to work, and a proportion of food shops are supposed to open.

But a trail around our usual local shops found only the excellent local bread shop to be open. And, in honour of the spring festival, there were two cashiers instead of the usual one. The shop had been split into two compartments, the first selling fresh bread, and the second selling the cakes and biscuits and sweets without which no Russian celebration is complete.

Around the corner, outside the shop that normally sells jams and tinned fruits, there was a small queue, which indicated special supplies. Once inside, the shop was crowded. Through the massed fur hats, we saw the oranges.

Not the small and mean apologies for oranges that you can sometimes buy from heaped crates outside the main metro stations, but huge and plump and marvellously vermilion things from Greece. At £2 a kilo they were ridiculously cheap.

They cost ten times as much in the free markets where the Georgian peasants sell their home produce.

And there were figs, fat and oozing with juice, at £1.80 a kilo, so we joined the queue.

We still had to find our butter, but none of the other shops seemed to be open, and then coming home through a side street, we came across a small shop, and we could see customers thronging inside. And through the condensation on the windows, we saw huge cheeses and bottles of Soviet champagne.

Two Russian women nearby went ahead and showed a small slip of paper to the white-coated woman who guarded the way in.

We slipped through after them, and stared amazed at the huge haunches of beef and pork, the lumps of fat bacon such as the Russians love.

Then the white-coated woman caught my arm. 'You are too young to have a pass, Comrade,' she said. 'This shop is not open to you.'

And indeed, all the shoppers were elderly, except for some young women carrying the bags for their parents. The white-coated lady broke off to check the passes of some more people.

We were about to leave, when the oldest lady of all painfully limped into the shop. She must have been a veteran of every great event of Russian history back to the first revolution of

1905. She showed no pass, but with the discretion that comes with years of practice, slipped a small anonymous parcel into the pocket of the guardian. 'You understand Citizenness,' she muttered. 'I have lost my pass. Just an accident.'

As we walked disconsolately back into the courtyard, we looked back and saw the old woman joining the queue for the bacon. The woman in the white coat glared at us, hands in pockets, as her fingers explored the shape of her bribe.

Birth of a nation
7 July 1986

There are some things about the Soviet Union that make me so angry I want to go and pelt the Kremlin with radioactive tomatoes. The latest infuriation is the cotton wool shortage.

This is not simply for the selfish reason that our family includes an infant who still wears nappies. It is because this vast continent of a country, this second most powerful economy in the world, does not produce tampons. And if it does manufacture sanitary towels they are virtually impossible to find, even in privileged Moscow.

In a country of almost 280 million people, getting on for a hundred million women are of child-bearing age. At any given time some ten million of them are menstruating. At a time of cotton wool shortage, what in the name of the Tsar of all Russia are they supposed to do about it?

The discomforts and humiliations to which this leads are bad enough. But it is worse than just a social and economic failure to provide for an elementary need of half the population. It is, in the plainest sense, an insult to Soviet women.

Nor is this spasmodic shortage of cotton wool an isolated example of a generally lamentable attitude towards women. This is a country where the standard form of birth control is abortion. I have yet to meet a Soviet woman who has not been through an abortion. One friend has had seven, and such are the rigours of the Soviet health service that each single time is etched in her memory as a grief and humiliation.

If you are lucky or well connected, you can obtain Hungarian and East German contraceptive pills. If you have had a child already, you can get fitted for an inter-uterine device. Some diaphragms are available, but one woman doctor of my acquaintance says, 'They come in two sizes – too big or too small.' And in the absence of spermicide creams, their reliability is sharply reduced.

There are condoms, and having examined the kind that are issued to Soviet soldiers, I can confirm the troops' suspicion that they are meant to double as galoshes or rainproof overtrousers. I would not be surprised to learn that they are bulletproof. The ones produced for the civilian market, Soviet friends tell me, will certainly tear during use, even if they are not holed already.

As a result, I was not in the least surprised to see that the London Rubber Corporation's profits have soared since I first came to Moscow. Every time I return, I cram the corners of my suitcase with packets of their gossamer products to pass on to my Russian chums. It also secures me the most awed glances as my baggage is searched at Soviet customs, but that is by the way. It is not easy to fathom why all this should be. A centrally planned economy, whose constitution gave women full legal rights rather earlier than most of the world, ought to be able to produce sufficient contraceptive and sanitary equipment to cater for the needs of its citizens.

Western cartoonists traditionally caricature frumpish Russian women cleaning the streets, building the roads and performing every kind of manual labour. They should not. This was largely the result of the war, and the desperate losses among men of working age.

What is more significant is the way that those professional jobs that women have come to dominate – they provide three-quarters of the doctors and two-thirds of the teachers – have suffered a sharp fall in status. They are among the lowest paid groups of Soviet society, earning about 70 per cent of the average industrial wage.

We are starting now to get the odd feminist stirring in Russia. The brave group of women in Leningrad who published the first feminist samizdat magazine have been exiled, but their cause goes on. At the recent congress of the Writers' Union, women asked why so few of them were represented on the ruling body, and indeed the poetess Bella Akhmadulina is now a secretary of the union.

Similar calls at the last party congress led to the election of Alexandra Bryukova as a full secretary of the Central Committee, the most powerful woman in Soviet life for a generation. Perhaps the second most powerful, if the widespread rumours of Raisa Gorbachev's influence on cultural reform are to be believed. But until you can buy Tampax anywhere in the country, I will remain sceptical of claims that the time of Soviet woman has come.

Second place
21 July 1986

Just beside the Moscow planetarium is a shop which somehow encapsulates the Gorbachev dilemma of how to revitalise this country's economy without dismantling the Soviet system.

It is a 'kommissioni', or second-hand shop, where the state buys and sells goods and takes a 7 per cent commission. It has also been for many years the focus of wealth-creation and social mobility in Moscow. This is the main kommissioni for electronic goods, from stereo tape decks to video recorders, and it was only when I discovered it that I began to learn how the Soviet system works.

Returning diplomats and officials who had been on foreign delegations would make a bee-line for this place almost as soon as they had cleared customs. The video recorder that cost them £350 in Britain would go on sale here at 6000 roubles or more. The stereo tape deck or the compact disc system or the Sony short-wave radio would command a proportionate mark-up.

Because of this, the permission for a Soviet citizen to travel abroad was like a licence to print money once they returned. And it was all entirely legal.

And it explained why the apartments of Muscovites who had often been abroad were much more lavishly equipped than those of people, even fairly senior officials who earned nominally far higher salaries, whose duties had kept them in the homeland.

When I first arrived in Moscow, this kommissioni was a thriving place, the counters crowded with people waving thick wads of roubles, and talking knowledgeably in Russian about the difference between Grundig and Panasonic, about Dolby systems and graphic equalisers and freeze frames and play-back speeds. The customers knew their stuff.

They also had the right to take an item home on approval for three days to see if it worked properly, before the deal was formally concluded.

All this has changed, since Gorbachev. It began with an experiment in a selected number of kommissioni shops, which has now been extended nation-wide. This permits no second-hand product to be sold for more than the new price of an equivalent Soviet product.

Then it rules that any item unsold after two weeks should be marked down by 20 per cent, and after another three weeks by 30 per cent.

The result was to empty the shelves of the kommissioni, as people stopped bringing their 'second-hand' goods for sale. But it has not stopped the business, which now takes place on the street outside the shop, or very discreetly through one or two of the more daring assistants who will put buyer and seller in private contact with each other, for a small commission on the eventual deal.

I tried this out the other day, went into the shop and looked at the sadly bare shelves, which contained two rather dowdy Soviet-made video recorders that have been nicknamed 'tape eaters'. I loitered, then waited in the street outside and a youth in jeans and leather jacket asked me if I were buying or selling.

'Selling a video. Panasonic,' I said. It is worth noting at this point the usefulness of the Soviet empire to a foreign journalist. My Russian is far too poor for a Russian-speaker ever to think of me as a fellow-national, but the people from the Baltic provinces often take a pride in their terrible mutilations of the Russian language. On a good day, I can pass for a short while as a Latvian.

We established that the video was almost new, that it could play Pal and Secam, and with the promise of throwing in four blank tapes I had an offer of 5000 roubles in cash. I then made my excuses and left, as they say. At the legal exchange rate, that is almost £5000.

The trade has not stopped. It has gone private. It has also gone effectively criminal, and the end of the three-day approval period means that the entire business is now wide open to fraud.

But there is no sign that any of this black-market activity is reducing. You can find a black market in computer parts and software outside the Pioneer shop on Gorky Street, and for electronic goods at the kommissioni shop, and for Western rock music tapes and records at the youth café on Leninski Prospect, all operating more or less openly.

It is the old story of supply and demand, and of human ingenuity outwitting the bureaucrat. And while one understands the distaste for the fast rouble that led the Gorbachev administration to clamp down on the kommissioni, one wonders at the lack of imagination that has simply moved the trade to the black market.

Night games
27 October 1986

Even in these days of glasnost in the Soviet press, with the once-forbidden topics of air crashes and ship collisions being reported alongside the corruption trials, the decision to air certain topics still comes as a shock.

Komsomolskaya Pravda is the official newspaper of the Young Communist League, and its long story, headlined 'A lady for a tip', raised many an eyebrow. Set in the Byelorussian capital of

Minsk, it recounted the stories of Svetlana, who sold her favours to the foreigners in the local Intourist hotel, and of Nina who ran a small brothel in a nearby apartment.

The main thrust of the article was to complain that in the absence of any Soviet law against prostitution, there was little social pressure that could be brought.

'Evidently there is no sense in agonizing over the social reasons for this phenomenon,' they had written. 'It is not poverty that makes these girls chase after their dubious clients. The majority of these "businesswomen" have a reasonably good education, some are fluent in foreign languages. Each one of them could be working for the good of society.

'In the old days, they would try to remain anonymous, and when caught, would promise never to do it again. But with the passing of time, this coyness has gone. They feel quite invulnerable, because they are breaking no laws. They exchange nods with the hotel doormen and greet the policemen in a friendly manner. In the hotel, the bar and the restaurant, they know everyone and everyone knows them. There is simply no public censure.'

When the police do bother to intervene, there are two laws they can use against the girls. The first is the law against being a social parasite, or against being unemployed. So the girls make sure they have a daytime sinecure, whether as a student or in a factory or shop where they can bribe the managers into turning a blind eye to their absences.

The second is the law against dealing in foreign currency. The girls *Komsomolskaya Pravda* is worried about are those who go with foreigners, and get their pay in dollars, finnmarks and pounds. Prostitution among Russians, which is widespread and visible in the big naval cities like Murmansk and Odessa, and around the hostels where Moscow's migrant workers live, has yet to emerge in the press as a social problem.

The odd thing about the article was why it chose to focus on Minsk, which is not on the main route for Western tourists or businessmen. Moscow provides far more glaring examples.

It can be embarrassing, for example, for Western women to try to go alone into the big hotels for foreigners. Unless they show a hotel residency card or a passport, they are liable to be turned away by the doorman, who will assume they are amateur whores.

The professionals are recognized and admitted, although I he was suddenly arrested by a team of men who had been waiting nearby. He was taken to Lefortovo prison and told he was under have on occasion seen the purple flash as a 25-rouble note changes hands. They dress well, in Western clothes brought in by their regulars, or bought in the hard currency stores. Many of them are stunningly attractive. Their hard sell and aggressive approach makes a quiet drink in these bars almost impossible. Prices, I am told, range from $50 to $100, and more for twosomes and special services.

The problem is that the price does not include the film and recording rights. Only a fool would ever assume that these hotel liaisons take place without an interested audience, or that the girls do not co-operate with the authorities when pressured to do so. There was the famous case of Commander 'Gunboat' Courtney, whose parliamentary career collapsed when photographs of his amorous adventure in a Moscow hotel suddenly appeared in the post of his constituency chairman.

There are other ways of applying pressure. A colleague of mine, a former *Newsweek* correspondent here, was suddenly informed by the foreign ministry that the Moscow VD clinic had been given his name as a contact by a hotel prostitute, and under Soviet law he had to be given a medical check and treatment.

Proclaiming his innocence to his embassy, he took the first plane to Frankfurt, had himself thoroughly checked there, and sent the papers proving his innocence, or at least his non-infection, back to Moscow.

He then flew on to New York, to explain to his employers why this had to be seen as a nasty attempt to discredit a thrusting and aggressive reporter, and to explain to his wife, who was having their first baby. Not as bad as the Daniloff case,* but a reminder that even gonorrhoea can be conscripted into the service of the Soviet state.

---

* Nick Daniloff was the Moscow correspondent for the weekly magazine *US News and World Report*. While going to meet a contact in a public place near a Moscow Metro station on 28 August 1986, he was suddenly arrested by a team of men who had been waiting

And now the bad news
3 November 1986

One of the most remarkable features of the campaign for glasnost in the Soviet media is that it has opened the columns of newspapers to the readers themselves. Readers' letters have always been a fascinating and important feature of Soviet papers, but increasingly we are now seeing new sections of the papers like 'What People Say' in *Moskovsky Komsomoletz*, or 'Brave And Honest Talk' in *Rabotnitsa*, the popular women's magazine whose circulation is 17.3 million.

And these sections are bringing into the public domain scandals that have long been kept quiet. I mention these two publications because each has recently published an astonishing letter about abortion, which is the Soviet Union's major form of birth control.

The first letter, in *Rabotnitsa*, cites a learned medical text, 'Demographic Factors of Health' for the chilling statistics that 70 per cent of urban women, and 90 per cent of rural women terminate their first pregnancy with illegal abortions; for girls up to the age of nineteen 87.5 per cent of them have their first abortion performed illegally.

The letter in *Moskovsky Komsomoletz* tells the tragic story of a sixteen-year-old girl who got pregnant. Her mother refused to help or even advise her to go to the state abortion clinic. She found an old woman who performed the abortion at home. Within four days, she was dead. The letter went on to cite five other fatalities from illegal abortions in that one small clinic in the past six months.

---

nearby. He was taken to Lefortovo prison and told he was under investigation for espionage. He was imprisoned for two weeks before being freed when mounting public and official anger in the US threatened to derail the progress in US-Soviet relations that had come with the Geneva summit of the previous year. Immediately Daniloff was freed and deported from the USSR, the Reykjavik summit was announced by the Kremlin and White House simultaneously.

I had come across this kind of story before, but through word of mouth. I had heard of one young woman who nearly died after trying to abort herself with a rubber galosh. 'I didn't boil it long enough,' she concluded. Another friend confided that she had been aborted by her aunt.

According to medical text in *Rabotnitsa*, one abortion in three is performed illegally in the Soviet Union mainly because the women need anonymity. A legal abortion in a state clinic means that a special medical licence for the time off will be sent to your place of work. 'Even if I write that the diagnosis is flu, my signature is so well known in this city, that the secret is soon out,' one abortion clinic doctor was quoted as saying.

Both letters agree that the soulless atmosphere of the state abortion clinics drives many women away. 'The first thing you see in the clinic is the big poster which warns: "Mother – do not kill your child,"' said the letter in *MK*.

'Women feel abandoned to indifference in the clinics. They need a human attitude, warmth and pity. But no one talks to them. There is an endless flood of patients, and sometimes they face real cruelty. There is a shortage of anaesthetics, so women must go without. We must humanize this operation,' the letter to *Rabotnitsa* argued.

Both letters pleaded for contraception to be made more easily available and more reliable. They argued for some sex education in schools so that teenage girls could learn how not to have babies rather than to be forced to abort them.

Significantly, the editorial board of *Moskovsky Komsomoletz* wrote a reply to the letter, broadly agreeing with its arguments. 'We are not in favour of premature initiation into intimate life for young people,' it began. 'But we should show understanding. To give birth or not must be for a woman to decide.'

There are two abortions performed for every live birth in the Russian republic, according to *Rabotnitsa*. This may explain the state's official discouragement of the practice, faced with a static population of Russians while the birth rate soars in the old Muslim republics of the south. Just over 75 per cent of Soviet women undergo abortions, *Rabotnitsa* went on, citing sociological surveys which I have not seen published before.

It is significant that the Soviet press is at last publishing information that was widely suspected before, but not openly discussed. But this new freedom to raise controversial topics has an odd side-effect.

The Soviet press seems suddenly full of bad news. The era of glasnost has brought us Chernobyl, and the drowning of over 400 people in the *Admiral Nakhimov* collision, plane crashes and detailed accounts of the breakdown of the Reykjavik summit. The cumulative effect of all this is depressing people almost as much as it liberates them. And it leaves a growing impression that whatever else you can say about Mikhail Gorbachev, he is unlucky.

Red sales after sunset
13 April 1987

As with several other Western correspondents here who seem to have become unpopular in certain quarters lately, I have just had my third flat tyre in less than twenty-four hours, which seems to be stretching the laws of coincidence rather far.

It was late in an evening when the Russian spring began to appear in a confused flurry of chill rain and wisps of snow, the kind of weather when taxis disappear as if by magic. I was far from a Metro station, and some distance from the tram routes. It was, all in all, the kind of situation that reduces people in the West to gibbering, manic frustration.

But this was Moscow, so I simply strolled to the edge of the road and stuck my hand out. A small Zhiguli drew up almost at once, the driver said he knew the way to Serpukhovsky Val, and we were off.

Moscow's unofficial taxi services are a tribute to the way people cope with the Soviet system. Over the past couple of years, I have been given lifts home by any number of private cars, an ambulance, a snow-clearing lorry, and even a police car.

We all had a nasty few weeks in the first summer of the Gorbachev regime when his economic reforms seemed to be more about discipline and cracking down on unearned incomes than about liberalization.

He had just announced the anti-alcohol drive, there was a new decree about registering every able-bodied Muscovite and making them show proof that they were gainfully employed, and then we got a new police regulation to stamp out 'unauthorised earnings' by the public. Their first target was the gypsy cabs, and late night transport became decidedly tricky.

No longer were most private drivers keeping a little pocket torch, with its glass screened by green paper, in the glove compartment. A little green light is the sign that a Soviet taxi is free for business.

But then things eased up again, with the Gorbachev statement that 'honestly-earned extra incomes' were a good thing for Soviet life, and the traffic police dropped their disagreeable habit of stopping cars at random and interrogating the passengers about their precise relationship to the driver.

When, the other evening, I asked my driver how he was prospering these days, he said, 'Ten times better than during the day. I'm an engineer, and you know they pay us a joke. I get 160 roubles a month, which makes a rouble an hour. Driving my car at night, I reckon to make 10 roubles an hour.'

It was the difference, he went on, between simply existing and being able to live a little. It meant spare cash to buy the expensive new kolbasa sausage, made of real meat, that you can get in the new co-op shops for about £11 a kilo. It also meant he could go on holidays to the Black Sea.

The factory where he worked was having a terrible time, with the new quality controllers rejecting half the small electrical generators that came off the assembly line. So there had been no bonuses paid this year, only the basic wage, and there had been a cut-back in the trade union vouchers for a subsidised three weeks at a holiday camp.

'So this year I'll be going Dikari,' he said, using the word which means 'savage' – the Russian slang for holidaymakers who rent rooms or beds in private homes in the resort towns, eat in restaurants or on the beach, and arrange their own train or air tickets to the sun.

Earning such a basic wage, how did he afford the car? 'It belongs to my father. He spent his savings on it, and he lets me use it in the evenings, if I get the petrol and do all the repairs. Five years old, and it isn't easy to keep it running. I can be off the road for a week to find a spare. You couldn't get a new battery anywhere in Moscow last winter. I finally got a train to Gorky and got one there from a friend.'

What worried him most was the need for new tyres. His current set were almost bald, and if he got stopped by the police they could order him off the road.

'You wouldn't have any spare tyres, for a good price?' he asked hopefully. No, I had a different kind of car, and although we foreigners could import new tyres from Finland, we had to pay 100 per cent customs duty on them.

'If you hear of any, give me a call,' he said. 'Or if you're going out and having a few drinks, give me a call and book me to pick you up. My dad will take the booking.'

He handed over a nicely printed card with his name and phone number and a little drawing of a Zhiguli car with a man waving from behind the wheel.

I gave him two roubles for the ride, and climbed out with a new respect for the small businessman in a hard climate.

Crime sheet
5 October 1987

It has been a quiet week on the crime front in Moscow, except for the case of the infected parrots.

Two cockatoos were stolen from the quarantine ward of the Moscow Zoo, where they were being treated for ornitosis, which is highly dangerous for humans. All visitors to the pet market should beware, in case the thieves try to sell the birds to an unsuspecting public. So said the lead item in the new weekly crime round-up in *Moskovsky Komsomoletz*, the paper of the capital's party youth organization.

Presented partly as a public service, partly as a proof of glasnost, it is also boosting the circulation of what in the past has been a fairly pedestrian publication. But then crime has not traditionally been a feature of the Soviet press.

Certain outstanding economic crimes used to get full publicity, if a proper ideological moral could be drawn. But *Moskovsky Komsomoletz*'s weekly grim catalogue of petty theft, muggings and murder is something new. Still, the economic crimes make interesting reading. Most foreigners visiting or living in Moscow have been pestered by the currency speculators and black market spivs who want to get into the 'beriozkas' – the hard-currency stores.

Last week they caught a chap called Zarubin while he was trying to buy beriozka cheques worth, it is said, 6000 roubles. If this refers to their street value on the black market, the cheques themselves may have had a face value of only 1500 hard currency roubles.

If he had cheques totalling 6000 roubles, the street value could have been as high as 30,000 roubles. With beriozka cheques, you can buy a bottle of vodka for 1.3 roubles, rather than the 10 roubles it costs in the usual shops. At Zarubin's home, police found and confiscated 50,000 roubles in used notes, and another 10,800 roubles of foreign currency cheques. From the way it was worded, this sounds like a wad of dough worth about 50,000 roubles on the street.

Then there was a report of a middle-aged worker committing suicide. But there were no details, no report of a coroner's inquest or any reason given. A little boy fell under the wheels of a tram. There was a photo of another little boy of about seven abandoned at a train station, and unable to give his name or address. Anyone who recognized him should get in touch with the police, the report said.

Another very Soviet kind of crime: a woman doctor was attacked by a mugger at 11 p.m. near her home. Her stolen bag contained blank forms for sick leave. They are worth money on the black market, too. The thief also took her umbrella.

The column reports another of the increasing attacks on cab drivers, and claims that there are now two a week.

Most Moscow cabbies will tell you there are far more than

that, and that they have their own list of no-go suburbs. This time, the cabbie was stabbed in the arm with a kitchen knife. The police caught the thief.

'The number of flat burglaries decreased somewhat, but there are still many of them,' the column said. 'It sometimes happens that burglars hit a particular flat six or seven times. But since the weather is turning cooler, many thieves and 'bomzhi' (people without a fixed address) have moved south to warmer climates. But burglaries remain a serious problem.'

Indeed they do. One of the thriving sectors in the newly-legalized private enterprise is that of the locksmiths. A full security job, with three separate custom-made locks that have not come from a state factory (whence thieves can easily obtain the basic lock patterns and designs) can cost 500 roubles. The growing popularity of good free enterprise locks has led to a nasty spurt in the incidence of lift-muggings, since it is now easier to hit victims outside their secure apartments.

This week, unusually, there was no mention of rape but most Moscow women will tell you that it, too, is on the increase. Sex did get a mention, in this form: 'A citizen of one of the African countries undergoing treatment for Aids simply walked out of the clinic. This was an open-type hospital without isolation precautions.'

End of story. Are we supposed to beware of black men? The thoughtlessness of Soviet reporting on Aids is alarming. So keen is it to stress that few Russians have been diagnosed as infected, and that it is mainly a foreigners' – and above all an African – problem, that the effect is unpleasantly racist. Or as my taxi driver said the other day; 'I won't have them in my cab, not with this Aids about.'

In the black
30 November 1987

It is the end of an era. One of Moscow's best-known black markets, the electrical goods secondhand store on the ring road by the planetarium, has been closed.

The shop itself is being refitted as one of the 'friendship' stores, the showcases for the Soviet colonies. This one is to be called Kabul, and will sell handicrafts and knick-knacks from Afghanistan.

Leather handbags, fur coats and jewellery made from cartridge cases, sniffed one Moscow friend. The real Afghan market will stay in Kabul. There are wonderful tales told back in Russia of the Afghan bazaar, and one acquaintance whose son did a tour of duty there showed me his Japanese stereo system and tape-deck that were brought back from Kabul. But this will not compensate for the loss of the Moscow kommissioni for electrical goods and cameras. It was not the goods offered inside that were the attraction, but the deals that could be made on the street outside, for videos, stereos, camera lenses and the like.

The Moscow black market has always been well-organized, and fairly predictable. The jewellery trade takes place outside the state's secondhand store by the Red Army park. It is just down the street from the place that sells the flat Georgian bread hot from the oven. And so, cash-rich from selling their fruit and flowers at the market, the Georgians head for some hot bread and then go buying gems.

The prices inside the store reveal just how much money is lurking in this superficially drab city. Last weekend, there was a diamond and sapphire necklace about 16,000 roubles, or about six years' pay at the average Moscow salary. My wife had hauled me along, not to buy, but to marvel at an antique necklace she had seen there a couple of days earlier priced at 35,000 roubles: it had already been sold.

This is the legal secondhand trade, where the goods are sold to the state shop, and then resold to the public at a standard 7 per cent mark-up. But human nature being what it is, choice goods bought by the store are often held back from the public counter, and made available, for an extra consideration, to the special customers.

This does not apply simply to the jewellery, but to the good fur coats in the secondhand clothes shops, to Western video systems, although their price has dropped by half in the last three years as the supplies have improved, and to the antique porcelain in the store by Oktyabraskaya Square. The black market operates by cutting out the middle man in the state store, intercepting the buyer before he gets into the store, or waiting for disappointed customers as they come out. And it is highly sensitive to fashion.

Ten years ago, the shop that is to be the 'Kabul' was one of the centres for the thriving trade in Western rock LPs and tapes, a market which has weakened with the growth of indigenous Soviet rock and the reduced jamming of Western radio stations.

The pace of change has been fastest at the informal market in computer goods outside the Pioneer shop on Gorky Street, where cassette computer games change hands for 200 roubles and more. Two years ago, there was a lively trade in the Polish copies of the now-ancient Spectrum personal computer, but then there was great excitement over the Soviet-made 'Agat' PC, which was said to be based on the architecture of the first Apple PCs. But the Agat has proved a disaster. The favoured experimental schools which had obtained the Agat complained that at any one time, half of them were out of order. The usual Soviet problems of quality control compounded fundamental design faults which made the Agat slow and cumbersome, with a complex programming style that actively discouraged novice users. Production was officially cancelled earlier this year. The new Soviet model, the 'Korvet', which is being turned out at a plant in Baku, is said to be more promising, but there are the usual massive delays in the provision of support systems, programmes and printers and extra memory.

But what can you expect from a computer industry whose organization is shared (according to *Pravda*) by five separate ministries, who depend on another thirty-two ministries for supplies and peripherals. So the Pioneer shop black market is now specializing in programmes for the 10,000 Japanese Yamahas that were imported for Soviet schools.

The good news is that a new electrical black market has emerged around another state secondhand shop opposite the Shabolovskaya Metro station. This weekend's prices were 3500 roubles for a Panasonic video recorder, and 250 roubles for a Russian-written chess-playing programme for an IBM clone. Forget Mikhail Gorbachev's perestroika: the black market will modernize this country yet.

'Ello, 'ello
21 December 1987

One of the disturbing and perhaps unexpected aspects of the
Soviet reforms has been the problem of what happens to large
numbers of crooked cops once they have been purged from the
police force. In the last years of Brezhnev, the Soviet police
were seriously bent. This was not just a question of everyone
carrying a five-rouble note in their driver's licence for the
traffic cops. The corruption went all the way up to the top. But
the purge, too, went all through the ranks, and in Gorbachev's
first few months in office, 40,000 pure young Komsomol
members and army conscripts were drafted into the force to
replace them. But what happened to the disgraced cops? Take
two humble examples, Igor Knigin and Valery Fineyev, who
worked in the Soviet version of the CID at Moscow's 114th
Militia Precinct.

'I joined the militia to fight crime, but then I discovered how
much of it was being organized in our police station,' Fineyev
later said at his trial. Knigin was one of the first organizers. His
first victim was the husband of his mistress, a man who
speculated in gold. Knigin arrested him, took him for a ride into
the country, robbed him, shot him twice in the head, and
buried him in a swamp. Detective Fineyev joined Knigin for the
second affair, a similar ride into the country for a drug dealer,
who managed to escape, and complained and appealed to his
local police chief for protection. Knigin was sacked from the
police, and Fineyev given a reprimand. But then Fineyev was
found to have beaten a false confession out of a prisoner who
had been accused of burglary.

That happened in 1984. 'At that time, this type of practice
was not forbidden,' *Komsomolskaya Pravda* reported. In 1985,
when Gorbachev came to power, the clean-up began. Fineyev
was given a three-year suspended sentence, which he served as
a gamekeeper. He was thus able to practise with firearms,
which was to come in useful.

His old chum, Igor Knigin, also needed a weapon. He
murdered another policeman on a late-night suburban train to

get his Makarov pistol. Knigin and Fineyev were then ready for the big one. They recruited two accomplices, an army officer, Yevgeny Subachev, who had access to more weapons, and another veteran of the security forces, Konstantin Golubkov, who had been sacked from the KGB in mysterious circumstances. (There has been no public announcement of a KGB purge, but Golubkov's dismissal lends some weight to the rumours.) Their target was Moscow's biggest department store, the Molodezhny. Fineyev dressed up in police uniform, and the other three waited in the car for the bank security truck to arrive to collect the store's takings. In the car with them they had two sawn-off shotguns, the Makarov, an American revolver, two grenades and three Molotov cocktails. These latter were for the police patrol car that should have been on the scene.

The guards came out with the day's takings, over 330,000 roubles. Two of the guards were shot dead on the spot, another was wounded, and an escorting policewoman was also killed with the shotgun. The gang fled with the money. Passers-by alerted another police car. It gave chase, and stopped the car. The gang came out shooting, wounding the two cops – and one of the robbers. It was the former KGB man, Golubkov. He was hauled, bleeding, back into the getaway car, where his accomplices shot him dead and tumbled his body out on to the street. The chase went on, with a city-wide police alert, and the escape car was finally blocked by a trolley bus outside the university Metro station. The crooks left the car and ran, as the police moved in. They caught Knigin, but he shot himself. Or that is what the trial record says.

The other two, Fineyev and the army officer, stayed on the run until the next day, after the police realized that Knigin was formerly one of theirs, and started chasing down his old buddies. When they came to look at the Makarov pistol with which Knigin had shot himself (and two cops, and the wounded KGB accomplice, and a security guard), they traced it back to the policeman who had been murdered on the suburban train. This was embarrassing. Two other men had already been tried and convicted for that murder. One was sentenced to death, the other to fifteen years. The case, mercifully, was under appeal and so the death sentence had not been carried out.

Fineyev has now in turn been sentenced to death. The army officer, Yevgeny Subachev, got ten years. He also suffered the ignominy of expulsion from the Communist Party. The money was all recovered. After the sentence is carried out, this affair will have claimed six lives, or eight, if you include Knigin's earlier victims. What alarms me is that there are at least another 40,000 other unemployed and crooked cops out there.

A soft shoe shuffle
4 January 1988

In the winter of 1941, when Hitler's armies were reeling back from Moscow in their first defeat, they declared an item of footwear a deadly weapon. The possession of valenki, the traditional Russian felt boots, was equivalent to the possession of a firearm and thus punishable by death throughout the Nazi occupied lands.

The Germans were not off their heads, or at least, not on this topic. Valenki allowed men to live and march and fight in the deep snow of a Russian winter. The German armies, ill-equipped for the cold, confiscated all the valenki they could find for their own men. They also knew that the only way Russian partisans could survive on the run and in the open forests, was with valenki.

They are giant boots made of vast amounts of crushed black felt that come up to your knee and make you look as if you have two broken legs and are wearing jet-black plaster casts. Indeed, the valenki help account for the monumental appearance of the Soviet traffic police who stay on duty throughout the coldest days. Valenki keep the feet warm and dry. In deep winter, when the snow has frozen, you can wear them anywhere. But in the early or late winter, when the snow is wet or thawing, you have to slip a pair of water-proof galoshes on to the feet to stop the felt from getting sodden and starting to rot.

My two daughters get through Western snow boots of high-tech nylon and space-age rubber composition in about two weeks flat. But when I was in deepest Siberia, in a country store patronized by Yevenk hunters who know a thing or two about the cold, I found a pair of valenki bootees just right for a three-year-old. That was one problem solved. But now the baby wears those, and the three-year-old is rather larger. So my wife has just qualified for the title of Moscow hero-shopper, because after fourteen stores, six hours of queueing and three ribs bruised from the skirmishing at the counter, she has come home triumphant with the light of battle in her eye and a new pair of small valenki, complete with galoshes.

Said like that, it sounds simple enough. You go to a store and say you would like a pair of valenki, and throw in a set of matching galoshes, please. Not in Moscow. They do not, as a matter of principle, sell the galoshes where they sell the valenki. Their manufacture is governed by different ministries, who neither co-ordinate their production plans (so there are always more, or fewer, galoshes than valenki) nor their retail distribution.

Thus to come home on the same day with valenki and galoshes in Moscow makes the achievements of the person who gets the mink coat for a fiver at Harrods annual sale pale into insignificance.

'The Germans used to kill for these things,' I told my wife. 'The Muscovites still do,' she replied, rubbing her bruises.

At the time, I was looking through *Izvestia*, and saw an interview with a trade ministry official who was wriggling under questions. 'The winter footwear and winter clothing deficits have been stabilized,' he said (which means they are now officially acknowledged to be permanent). He claimed that overall they were managing to supply about two thirds of the national needs, but *Izvestia* pointed out that 'in such items as fur coats for children, fur boots, muskrat hats, natural fur coats and valenki, the supply is practically zero.'

This is the kind of shortage that Gorbachev's economic reforms are supposed to put right, but the journal *Sotsialistich-eskaya Industria* ran a survey on the progress of reform in the Russian clothing industry, and found that this year production was over 361 million roubles down on last year. At say 100 roubles for a coat, that means 3,610,000 fewer coats.

The reason for the fall is Gospriomka, the new quality control board which is rejecting sub-standard goods as they come off the assembly lines. This means the workers do not get their bonuses for fulfilling the plan. And, of course, even as wages come under pressure, prices are rising. To quote the same paper, 'prices are shocking many buyers. An autumn/spring coat now costs as much as we used to pay for a winter coat, while these now cost as much as luxury items, even while it is a necessity in our climate.' A heavy woollen winter coat for a man will cost at least 200 roubles – the average monthly salary in Moscow. A pair of reasonably fashionable boots for women will cost 160 roubles and more. My rabbit-skin fur hat cost 14 roubles three years ago, but these days, a worse quality 'shapka' will set you back 25 roubles.

But the children's valenki were a bargain at 7.25 for the boots, and an extra 1.25 for the galoshes. However, since the kids will now be able to spend all day skiing and sledging, my problem is to find some valenki in my size.

Hot blood, cold climate
March 1988

This may be a sign of curious perversion, but I find Russian winters rather erotic. It is something to do with women's eyes, which are usually the only feature you can see as they wrap up against the cold in thick fur collars and hats.

The eyes of Russian women flash in a quite remarkable way. They tend to have plumply rounded cheeks, pale skin and delicate small noses, and to trudge through the snow is to experience a constant barrage of their twinkles and gleams and mysteriously penetrating looks.

It is all quite harmless, a matter of the briefest eye contact that is in no way an invitation to stop and converse, still less to plough through the layers of winter clothing to the woman underneath. But there is something more sensual, more exciting, in these bright eyes flashing through the snow than any number of bikinis on beaches.

Eyes are ageless. These bold visual challenges can come from grandmothers and schoolgirls alike, from women whose waddling walk suggests an ungainly dumpling beneath the coat, to the sveltest of Svetlanas.

There is something quite magical about this. Many Russian girls, when you see them indoors, have a characteristic colouring of white skin, very pale blue eyes and wispy blond-white hair that makes them look seriously anaemic. But wrap them in fur and clap a winter 'shapka' on their heads, and the eyes suddenly blaze out fiercely, dark and strong.

Russians will tell you that there is a reason for the endless celebration of Russian eyes in poetry and prose. They say that it comes from the habit of tightly swaddling Russian babies, wrapping their little limbs so closely that they learn to communicate with their eyes alone, flashing invitations from the very cradle.

There are other sensual pleasures of winter. There are few sensations that so combine heat and cold as kissing the super-chilled cheeks of a woman who has been walking in temperatures of 20°C below freezing. And there are few scents quite so intoxicating as the freshness of a woman coming in from the cold.

But the great mystery to me is what on earth the Russians do about this constant current of deep-frozen eroticism. The Soviet Union is officially a rather straight-laced society. Casual sexual encounters are not encouraged by the system.

Amorous Russians cannot quickly check into a hotel, not without showing the papers that say they are married. And the Soviet housing shortage is a far more effective prophylactic than any passing worries about Aids.

Human nature being what it is, solutions have been found. One, or rather two, can take a night train to Leningrad or the Baltic city of Tallin, booking one of the soft class two-berth cabins. In summer, there are the river steamers, again with two-berth cabins.

This can be fun. The bunks are so narrow and the train ride so bumpy that anything more than the most casual amorous dalliance requires a sense of balance and a readiness to undertake strenuous physical contortions. But tickets for two on a night sleeper cost over 60 roubles, or a week's average pay. It is not, therefore, a common resource. And that great stand-by of Western courtship, the car park, is less than attractive in a society where cars are few and the outside temperature low enough to freeze the locks, if not the passions.

From my own strolls through parks and countryside, I can confirm that the Russians are among the world's most enthusiastic practitioners of the splendid art of love-making in the open air. Indeed, in the long grass of Izmailovo Park last summer, a friend of mine was flying a kite and broke his leg when he tripped over one enraptured couple.

But a superhuman degree of passion is required for alfresco frolics between November and March, and so the perennial lovers' question of finding somewhere to be alone has a particular intensity in Russia.

They are not a prudish people. They could not be, speaking a language so marvellously rich in earthy jokes and bawdy oaths. So flats and spare rooms and dachas are made available and borrowed among friends almost as a matter of course.

But probably the majority of young Russian single people, whether students or young workers, tend to live in hostels and dormitories, where real privacy can seldom be found. There is no single Russian word that can be translated as 'privacy'. There are circumlocutions about the state of being alone, and the privacy of thought has to be expressed in Russian as one's secret thoughts. And so I was not over-surprised when a straw poll of those friends to whom I am close enough to ask about this sort of thing, found that only one in four had not at some point made love in public, or with only a thin curtain around the bed to shield them from others in the same room.

This must mean silent love-making, I observed to one chum. Who needs to speak, when it can all be said in the eyes, came the unanswerable reply.

2
People

Journalism is based on generalizations which we cannot do without. But they are never entirely correct and are often misleading. So this is an attempt to correct the balance a little by writing about some individuals, and how their lives work.

A green among Reds
14 July 1986

Valentin Rasputin is not only one of the outstanding Soviet writers, he is a political phenomenon. But I was struck the other day when I had the pleasure of meeting him by the overpowering shyness of the man.

He is one of nature's self-effacers, hesitant and almost painfully polite. He has homely squashed-in features, and speaks in a quiet but terribly fast monotone. To meet him, you would not think that Valentin Rasputin is in large part responsible for the fact that we can now speak of such a thing as Soviet public opinion without mockery.

Now nearly fifty, he lives in his native Siberia, the setting of most of his books, near the shores of the Lake Baikal whose purity he has fought to defend. And his campaigns in letters to the press, in short stories and in his novels, have not only made him a one-man Greenpeace in the Soviet Union. They have forced the authorities to take notice, and indeed now to put him on the commission which is assessing the lake's future.

'It used to be the era of the poet, then of the novelist, and now it is the age of the publicist,' he says. 'We need the publicist against the growing possibility not just of physical extinction, but of spiritual extinction. Writers cannot keep silent on the great questions of good or evil.'

When one hears a Soviet writer say this kind of thing, you expect an instant follow-up on the beauties of the Soviet disarmament proposals and the stubborness of the West failing to agree. Not with Rasputin. He goes on to complain of the traditional lack of civic activity among his Russian people (he never talks of them as Soviet), and to hammer again at the theme of the pollution of Lake Baikal.

And when he is not fighting for the lake which provides the world's largest reserve of fresh water, he is fighting the proposal to reverse the flow of the Siberian rivers.

These campaigns flow naturally from the themes of his novels, which defend the old ways of peasant Russia against a soulless Soviet modernity. My own favourite is *Farewell to Matyora*, the last days of an old village that is being flooded by the rising waters of the huge dam that will feed the Bratsk power station.

In Soviet mythology, Bratsk dam is one of the looming symbols of modernity, of the success of communism in taming nature and putting the power of Siberia to work for man. Rasputin's novel is, in this sense, deeply and movingly subversive.

The novel is overwhelmed by the old women of the village, their memories and their sense of an ancient, sound and honourable culture being raped and desecrated. The key confrontation comes when the work crews arrive to clear away the old village cemetery and its crosses.

'People have forgotten their place under God,' says old Detya to her keen young grandson.

Most of Rasputin's stories cover this kind of theme, whether a sympathetic portrait of a wartime deserter who goes home to his village and his barren wife, or the tale of a hapless and barely literate rural woman who loses a thousand roubles from the till of the little shop she is assigned to run.

Rasputin is not alone in this kind of theme. Indeed, the village school of novelists is probably the healthiest and most

impressive in the current 'approved' canon of Soviet literature, and their theme goes far beyond nostalgia. There is
bitterness for the loss of the old communities, and a fairly
evident loathing for the Soviet collectivization that has replaced
them.

Occasionally, the theme is taken further, and Vasil Bykov's
recent interview in *Literaturnaya Gazeta* was unprecedented
in the way it publicly raised the forbidden topic of those
Soviet peasants who welcomed the Nazi invaders in 1941,
because of the way they had been demoralized by Stalin's
collective farms.

But Rasputin's constant public espousal of ecological causes,
his hammering away at the spiritual losses which he believes
endanger the very identity of the Russian people, is even more
remarkable. And his latest campaign promises to continue in
that astonishing Russian tradition of author as preacher and
moral arbiter which has been a current throughout Russian
letters from Tolstoy to Solzhenitsyn.

'We must have a national organization for ecology with
greater prestige and authority than any official body in the
state,' he demands. But when this shy little man from Siberia
gets an idea in his head, people start to pay attention. Just ask
those Soviet planners who began polluting Lake Baikal and
dreamed of reversing the Siberian rivers.

Ovir to you Mikhail
15 June 1987

Little Nathan Danovich is going on his first demo today, and
he is just three months old. He will probably spend it asleep, in
his mother's arms, on the steps of the Lenin Library just
opposite the reception office of the Supreme Soviet.

His sister Lilia will be there. She is seven. And his father will
probably have to sit on the steps because he is on hunger strike
for the right to go to Israel.

Their case is common enough. They first applied to go to Israel in the summer of 1983. In the autumn of 1984, the Israeli Knesset confirmed that the Danovich family had been granted Israeli citizenship, and then the family began the long process of applying to leave the Soviet Union, and to surrender their Soviet citizenship.

In the absence of any reply from Ovir, the immigration department, they wrote letters of appeal to the minister of the interior, to the general prosecutor, to Mikhail Gorbachev, and to the main newspapers. The only replies they received said that their inquiry had been passed to the Ovir office, which still insisted that no decision had yet been made on their case.

In March of this year, they appealed formally to the Supreme Soviet, having exhausted all other avenues. At the end of May, having had no reply, the Danovich family wrote to the Supreme Soviet to inform them officially that they had no alternative but to make a public demonstration.

Those are the bald facts of the matter, and stories such as this are now so common among Soviet Jews that they no longer make big headlines in the West. Which means that Western correspondents in Moscow do not go out of their way to cover their plight, as we did in the 1970s. Quiet and dignified demos are becoming less of a rarity in Moscow, and it is only when the security forces lose control, or stage a violent demo of their own as they did in Moscow's Arbat last February, that the story manages to cut through the general air of glasnost that now dominates our reports.

That veteran human rights campaigner, Dr Andrei Sakharov, perhaps made more of a stir when he button-holed Jacques Chirac just before the French premier went into the Kremlin for his talks with Gorbachev. The releases of prisoners of conscience had stopped, Sakharov said. He knew of just over a hundred who had been freed, which meant more than a thousand were still inside.

A cynic would say that Mr Gorbachev had got his world headlines from freeing Dr Sakharov from exile in Gorky, from freeing just over a hundred people who should never have been imprisoned anyway, and from promises of more Jewish emigration.

A cynic would not necessarily be right. Emigration visas for

Soviet Jews are now at the highest level since the 1970s. And a candidate member of the Politburo, former culture minister Piotr Demichev, now chairs a special commission of the Supreme Soviet which reviews the cases of Jewish emigration and of prisoners of conscience, and even has the right to over-rule the ministry of the interior when it recommends that someone should not be allowed to go.

And there are counter-pressures. The Syrians and other Arab friends have made it clear that a new round of mass emigration of Soviet Jews to Israel would not be well-received in the Arab world. Foreign policy advisers point out that with a Soviet-sponsored international peace conference on the Middle East becoming likely, and with the re-opening of diplomatic relations with Israel now firmly on the agenda, any gestures on Soviet Jewry could usefully wait awhile.

This is the realpolitik of human rights, the Soviet Union turning the West's strategy of linking human rights concessions to arms and trade agreements back upon us.

And in the meantime, I am sitting in a small flat with the Danovich family, watching a man preparing to risk himself and his family, to take a three-month-old babe in arms to a demonstration in a police state.

You can smell fear in a man, and you can sense resolution. And there are both in this calm-faced man as he strokes blunt fingers through his beard and tells me how he taught himself Hebrew, which is the language he wants his children to grow up speaking. We have made human rights into politics. But it always comes down to this, the decision of a fellow human being to meet head-on a state machine that is both bigger and less human than he. For a journalist, the hard part is to watch that decision being made and to cover its consequences. Spare a thought for baby Nathan this morning, and for his father.

Vassily Holmes
17 August 1987

Not long after I first arrived in Moscow, I was lucky enough to meet Vassily Livanov, a man with perhaps the best-known voice in the Soviet Union – a cross between Marlene Dietrich on heat and the slow pouring of gravel.

I used to assure that its timbre came from his habit of chain-smoking Herzogovina Flor, the Balkan cigarettes Stalin used to crumble into his pipe. But Vassily stopped smoking last year and his voice is unchanged.

You hear it on almost every Soviet children's cartoon, and a generation of young people have grown up convinced that their heroes speak this way. Ever since Vassily became the Sherlock Holmes of Soviet TV, one of the most successful series ever screened here, all the grown-ups know him too.

They do a marvellous job of recreating Victorian London by shooting at selected locations in Leningrad and Riga, and Vassily is the most convincing Holmes I have seen.

We became friends over a convivial lunch at the Writers' Club in Moscow, in the vast dining-room which Tolstoy describes in the masonic scene in *War and Peace*. It turned out that we shared a fondness for Rudyard Kipling: Vassily declaimed Fuzzy-Wuzzy in Russian and I chimed in with the English in what has now become our party trick.

Vassily's father was one of the best-known pre-war Soviet actors and worked with Stanislavski. The family apartment off Gorky Street is a veritable museum of Soviet theatre, and Vassily's dacha, on a riverbank about twenty miles from Moscow, is one of my favourite places.

As well as acting, writing wonderful children's stories, and producing a film about his father's life, Vassily now has a new interest. His *Sherlock Holmes* series has become a cult among Soviet detectives and he has the backing of the MVD, the Ministry of the Interior, to open a new theatre in Moscow that will be uniquely independent of the Ministry of Culture.

Sponsored by the MVD, the 'Detective' Theatre will present only whodunits and mysteries, and Vassily has now got me trawling through my paper-backs to find plots that can be adapted for the Soviet stage.

It was through this connection that I came across one of the most bizarre developments of the new freedom for private enterprise. The Soviet Union is about to have its first private detectives. The idea is they should track down missing persons, or look for husbands who have stopped paying alimony, or for runaway children who are beyond an age where the police take much interest.

It is an open secret that some policemen have undertaken this kind of work in their spare time for many years, moonlighting as private eyes. But legitimizing the profession will now involve getting a special licence, and working under a code of conduct.

Most investigators in the Soviet police go into the job after graduating as lawyers, and some of Vassily's lawyer friends see a bright future.

I suspect that one factor behind this new interest is the massive popularity of the novel *The Sad Detective*, by Viktor Astafyev, which began appearing in serial form in the magazine *Oktyabr* last year.

There is no real plot, simply the sad, unfolding life of a forty-two-year-old detective who has retired from the police as an invalid after being badly wounded. He lives in a grim provincial town and, even though trying to build a new life as a writer, keeps meeting muggers, drunks and petty criminals and sad, low-life losers, characters who have traditionally not been allowed into Soviet literature.

'When I was in the police, I used to think there were two worlds, the criminals and law-abiders, and our job was to keep them apart. Now I know you can't. It is one world,' the hero observes at one point.

The book was widely criticized as negative and wilfully depressing, painting too black a portrait of Soviet life, un-redeemed by the positive-thinking hero that socialist realism traditionally has required. Until Gorbachev and glasnost, it would have had little chance of being published.

But the main reason for the book's popularity, apart from the whiff of scandal attached to it, was the almost Don Quixotian portrait of the sad detective himself. It reminded me of Raymond Chandler's definition of the private eye as battered knight errant, soldiering on through disillusion and betrayal, maintaining a lonely integrity. 'Down these mean streets a man must go . . .' and all that.

Vassily's success could be that he plays Sherlock Holmes in precisely this way. The persistence of this human archetype, from Victorian Britain through Chandler's Los Angeles to Gorbachev's Moscow, even after fifty years of socialist realism, is one of those reassuring things about the human race and what we all have in common.

Games show

24 August 1987

Yuri Chernavsky and I first met a year ago, in the noisy communal flat in Moscow's Baumanskaya district where he has lived for years. About one Moscow family in six lives in the communal apartments which for decades have been the Soviet answer to the housing shortage, with four or five families decanted into a large apartment, sharing the kitchen and bathroom. In Yuri's case, there was a great deal more noise than usual.

He showed me his studio – a small room with a high ceiling, packed with Moog synthesisers, tape-decks, amplifiers, multi-channel mixers and, in a corner screened off by sound baffles, a microphone and music stand. Yuri is the leading Soviet composer of electronic music – not your Stockhausen, but the popular stuff. He came to prominence when he wrote the signature tune for last year's Goodwill Games, which reminded me of 'Chariots of Fire' written for troikas.

He is about to become even better known, because he has established the first legal independent record label in Soviet history. He has signed a contract with Melodiya, the state recording monopoly, that means it will press and distribute one record a month from his stable.

But the deal Yuri has negotiated means rather more than just producing occasional records. He has set up an organization known as the Studio of Popular Music. In terms of legal structure, it owes something to the new privileges that the Gorbachev reforms give to co-operatives, and something to the new licence for modest private enterprise.

The idea is to produce a miniature Soviet version of a Western record company that finds new talent, trains it, packages and manages it, finds the right music, arranges it for the band, records it, and then promotes the overall package and plans its TV and concert performances. Instead of a single hit record, the result is a successful cultural institution, a string of Soviet Abbas.

It is all very ambitious and a strikingly new concept in the Soviet Union. Yuri has spent the past six months selling the idea to Melodiya, the state broadcasting system, the Musicians' Union and all of the other Soviet bureaucracies who hitherto have seen one of their duties as stopping this sort of free-wheeling and independent initiative from ever getting under way.

But it is not quite independent. The Soviet system, even under the Gorbachev reforms, does not work that way. Yuri's studio is linked to another new organization, the Sport and Entertainment Organization. It is a belated admission by the Soviet system that, in the media age, the two things go together.

The experience of the Goodwill Games, held in Moscow last year and sponsored by the Turner Broadcasting Corporation, and the earlier example of the highly commercial Los Angeles Olympics, inspired some rather creative thinking in the Soviet Sports Committee. Recently it announced plans to build a golf and country club outside Moscow to host the New Soviet Masters' Golf tournament, with a prize of $100,000. Now this new sport and entertainment organization is preparing to stage a lavish floor show at the next Winter Olympics in Canada.

Soviet gymnasts and dancers had been staging this kind of thing for years. The Moscow Olympics and the Goodwill Games saw massed dances and geometric displays that made you think the top drill squad of the Coldstream Guards had suddenly donned tutus and track suits and borrowed some routines from the old Hollywood musicals.

Anyone who saw the opening ceremonies of the Games on TV will recall the dancers suddenly quick-stepping to form the letters USSR, and cartwheeling away to reform in the shape of a hammer and sickle. Now it is going commercial, and Yuri has managed to insert his own operation into the overall scheme.

He does not look like a pop promoter, being skinny and lugubrious and wearing thick-lensed glasses. But in musical terms, he has a sharp commercial brain. His pop song 'Banana Islands' would have done well in the Western charts, and some of his longer, electronic pieces reminded me of Mike Oldfield, only not so laid back.

I have few doubts about Yuri's chances of bringing off this grandiose scheme. The equipment in his studio was mainly Japanese, and the skills that went into acquiring it will serve him well in the new venture. But that is the curious thing about the whole thrust of the Gorbachev reforms.

All the entrepreneurial skills and the kind of creative individuality which used to be frowned on by the Soviet system are now becoming the best hope that it can relax and prosper and grow in the way that Gorbachev seems to want. If it gets Yuri out of the communal flat and into his own pleasant co-operative apartment, so much the better.

Stars and scars

28 September 1987

I called in the other day to interview Professor Svyateslav Fyodorov, the pioneering eye surgeon. By chance, it was the day he had been to the Kremlin to receive his gold star as a Hero of Socialist Labour from President Gromyko, a grand and informal occasion which was screened that evening on the TV news. The red-ribboned star gleamed in its box as we spoke in his crowded office.

It was the very picture of 'perestroika', of purposeful work and high tech as the huge conference table filled up with the new surgical tools his technical team had developed – scalpels one-tenth the thickness of a razor blade, minute gold implants to re-shape the cornea. Behind him, closed-circuit colour screens showed operations in progress in the production-line operating theatre upstairs, five sets of hugely magnified eyes being operated on simultaneously by five surgeons seated above the conveyor belt that rolled the patients along.

Then another visitor arrived, a journalist from Kiev who had found in some archive a photograph of the professor's father, dating from 1937. We watched Fyodorov gaze reverently at the tiny snapshot. It had been taken the year before his father, a cavalry division general, was arrested in Stalin's purge of the officer corps.

'He stayed in the camps for eighteen years,' said the newly-honoured hero of the Soviet state. 'When the Germans invaded in 1941, Marshal Timoshenko came to Stalin with a list of 120 senior officers who had been arrested, but not shot, and pleaded with him that the country needed their military skills,' he said quietly. 'Stalin went down the list, which was in alphabetical order, ticking off the names. But he decided he had to stop somewhere, and near the end of the list, he stopped.

'My father's problem was that his name began with F, which is at the end of the Russian alphabet. In the camp in Siberia, he said goodbye to friends who had been freed to fight the Nazis, but he had to stay, just because of a surname.'

All the time he spoke, he stared fixedly at the photograph of his handsome father, who looked amazingly young for a general. And I thought of how many other people I had met, now valued and honoured by the Soviet state, who had this personal memory of the purges, this reason to loathe a system that could do that to so many of its people, and yet who remained loyal and had been of great service to the state.

I thought of Vladimir Karpov, whom I had come to know when he was editing *Novy Mir*, the literary magazine. He is now the secretary of the Writers' Union, a candidate member of the Central Committee. He too, wears the gold star of a hero of the Soviet Union, which he won in the field for creeping behind German lines to take prisoners.

They called these prisoners 'yazyki', or tongues, and the usual rule was that you won the hero medal for twenty successful missions behind the German lines. Karpov brought back seventy-three before getting his award, because he was serving in a penal battalion, having been brought back from the gulag in order to fight. His crime had been to say to a fellow officer cadet at his military school: 'Stalin, Stalin. That's all we ever hear about. Does nobody talk of Lenin any more?'

We still do not know exactly how many victims Stalin claimed in his purges, nor how many died in the famines that attended his collectivization of the farms, nor how many served time in his prisons. One figure that I tend to believe was quoted by Anton Antonov-Ovseyenko in his book *The Time Of Stalin*, published by Harper and Row in New York in 1981. His father had been the man who led the charge on the Winter Palace in 1917, an honoured old Bolshevik who had been sent as Soviet ambassador to Madrid in the Spanish Civil War, where he helped administer the purges there before being summoned home to Moscow to be purged in his turn.

His son claims to have seen the secret report on Stalin's terror that was prepared by the Central Committee after Stalin's death. This was based on the records of the Lubyanka prison, which was the administrative centre of the purge, and which allegedly recorded 18,840,000 arrests in the six years after 1935 – or about 10 per cent of the population.

Even without this 'evidence' I reckon about one in three of my Russian friends have personal experience of the horror of it all in their own families. And they make up, on the whole, a vital part of the constituency for reform, for a truthful Soviet history which will record what Stalin did to them, and who want some simple acknowledgement of the need for a belated justice.

3

High Arts

The Soviet state is very proud of its showcase arts, its élite companies like the Bolshoi and Kirov ballets, the MKhAT (or Moscow Arts) and Taganka theatres, and of the country's classic traditions in literature and music and art. It has every right to be. This is a culture which produced Tolstoy and Pushkin and Dostoievsky, and Tchaikovsky and Shostakovich, and which boasts the world's richest single museum in the Hermitage.

But it is also the philistine state machine which bullied and abused Shostakovich, which killed its poets like Gumilyov and Mandelshtam, and which imprisoned and exiled Solzhenitsyn and Ratushinskaya.

The most exciting, because most dramatic and most immediate, feature of the Gorbachev revolution was the cultural thaw. But it was not universally welcomed. The price of persecuting people like Solzhenitsyn was that party hacks and time-servers were officially hailed as great men of Soviet letters. The most blatant example was the way that the self-serving and mendacious memoirs of the semi-literate Leonid Brezhnev won the state prize for literature. The cultural thaw meant that the game was up. It threatened the privileges of those who had done well out of the philistine ascendancy, and they fought it and delayed it with their own unique and outstanding skill – bureaucratic cunning.

It would be tempting to say the cultural thaw was the good guys versus the bad, the freedom-loving artists against the party apparatchiks. It was never quite that simple. Personal feuds and historic enmities intervened, and there was no guarantee that the political reformers were great artists. So these articles are reports from an uncertain battlefront, where the skirmishing goes on. And the best hope that the good guys may eventually win this 'war for the Soviet soul', as Yevtushenko once described it, is that the rude energy and exuberance and dubious taste of the Low Arts may yet come to the rescue of the High.

The write stuff
19 June 1986

A small reshuffle at the Kremlin during yesterday's session of the Supreme Soviet has aroused hopes among Soviet writers and artists that the party's traditional grip on cultural life could be relaxed.

Pyotr Demichev, the chemical engineer and former head of the Moscow City Party, has been minister of culture since 1974, and he was yesterday moved upstairs to the mainly ceremonial post of Deputy President of the Praesidium. He replaced Vasily Kuznetsov, eighty-five, the oldest in the Soviet Leadership, who retired on pension.

Demichev had a singularly uninspired reign as culture minister and the rumours of his departure have been current for some months, and recounted with heartfelt glee by many of Moscow's leading cultural figures. His main task was to keep the lid on the bubbling pot of literary dissidence and samizdat publishing, an unpleasant task which he performed without apparent relish or regret.

But the pot has shown signs of boiling over again in recent months. The new wave of literary impatience with censorship and the continuous taboo on writing about vast swathes of Soviet history began last year, with the celebrated speech of the poet Yevgeny Yevtushenko to the Russian Writers' Union. He said, in effect, that an honest Soviet Union depended on honest artists and writers, and until they explore Stalin's crimes as well as his achievements, they could hardly claim to be honest.

Yesterday, *Literaturnaya Gazeta*, the organ of the Writers' Union, published two articles by eminent authors which fully endorsed Yevtushenko's argument. This was the more significant, because yesterday also marked the fiftieth anniversary of the death of the revered writer Maxim Gorky, the father of the socialist realism school of writing, and it was also the issue looking forward to next week's key conference of the all-Soviet Writers' Union.

Vyacheslav Kondratiev, who made his name with novels of the war, complained of the censors whose new obsession with the anti-alcohol campaign was leading them to cut references to the historic fact that Soviet assault troops were given a slug of vodka before an attack.

This campaign against the political masters of culture has been gathering pace for some time. Last February, the poet Andrei Voznesensky fulminated in *Sovietskaya Rossiya* against the way that 'an author spends 10 per cent of his life on writing, and 90 per cent on getting it published.'

The latest issue of *Sovietskaya Kultura* this week published the posthumous notes of Konstantin Simonov, and focused on the draft of a speech he wanted to give at a Writers' Union conference in 1973. 'We need to remove the blank spots from our literature and history,' he said, and listed some banned writers whose works should be made available.

This ferment in the literary world has its echoes in other fields. At the conference of Soviet composers in April, the chairman of the Russian composers board, Rodion Schedrin, launched an extraordinary public attack upon the deputy minister of culture, Georgy Ivanov, condemning him as a bad administrator who also knew nothing of music.

In the theatre too the same points are made. Andrei Goncharov, director of Moscow's Mayakovsky Theatre, published a strong statement in *Sovietskaya Kultura* which said, 'I want to add my voice to those friends and colleagues who say that it is no longer possible to live in the way our theatre is functioning now ... we cannot even decide which plays we want to put in our repertoire.'

Next week's writers' conference is evidently shaping up to be a remarkable event, and the removal of Demichev from the Ministry of Culture has given the campaigners a kind of official endorsement. Certainly, they feel that the new leadership in the Kremlin is on their side.

Not only is Mikhail Gorbachev a man of Yevtushenko's and Voznesensky's generation, he is the first Soviet leader since Lenin who mixes privately with writers and artists.

Indeed, one of his aides is the journalist and playwright Fyodor Burlatsky, whose play *Burden of Decision* has been one of the hits of the season. Based on the Cuban missile crisis, it portrayed President Kennedy in a remarkably sympathetic light.

The reformers may yet be disappointed. The new minister of culture has yet to be named. But with the heavy-weight literary magazine *Novy Mir* publishing this week a long account by Ginghiz Aitmatov of his fictional forays among Soviet drug-addicts and the hash smokers, some recognition of the cultural revolution has already arrived.

Query about Tolstoy
8 December 1986

Soviet officials can be as 'economical with the truth', to borrow Sir Robert Armstrong's ringing phrase, as British civil servants. But in my experience they very rarely tell a downright public lie. So let us nail one here.

On the recent occasion of the founding of the Soviet Cultural Fund, which cynics have unworthily described as a job creation scheme for Mrs Gorbachev, a press conference was held in Moscow. I asked the question whether, in view of the widespread Russian and international concern over the threat of industrial pollution to Tolstoy's home at Yasnaya Polyana, the Fund's spokesmen were satisfied with the current strength and reach of their laws to protect historic monuments. And if they were not, would the fund campaign to strengthen them?

The question was answered by one Gennady Myasnikov, described as the deputy chairman of the Cultural Fund.

I was chided. My question was improper. Was I not aware that a special decision had been adopted by the Council of Ministers to give Yasnaya Polyana particular protection? There were no more problems at the delightful leafy estate where the father of Russian letters lies buried.

This was quite simply untrue. The newspaper *Sovietskaya Rossiya* has recently devoted a long article to Dmitry Likhachev, the grand old man who is the chairman of the Cultural Fund, and who also sat at the podium at that press conference. The article dealt with Likhachev's mail, and quoted particularly concerned letters from the public about Yasnaya Polyana.

'Despite numerous assurances and official statements that the situation is improving there, various administrative buildings keep mushrooming on the estate. Within 200 yards of Tolstoy's grave they are building a new heating station. One of the famous leafy alleys through the park has been covered with concrete ...'

The first official decree on the need to preserve and protect Tolstoy's old estate was signed in 1921. But then came the Azot industrial complex, a huge fertilizer plant within sniffing and poisoning distance of Yasnaya Polyana.

In the years 1953–65, and 1974–79, periods which coincided with the expansion of the plant, 'mass death of valuable trees took place at Yasnaya Polyana', according to *Sovietskaya Rossiya*.

The Council of Ministers indeed passed a special decree in 1983 declaring the place 'a spiritual holy place for the Soviet people', and demanding 'urgent measures to prevent air and soil pollution'.

The Ministry of Mineral Fertilizers, which is responsible for the Azot plant, was instructed to reduce their emissions, and to install purifying filters.

They have not done so. Indeed, the factory's latest plans call for an increase in production, no cut in atmospheric emissions, and there are no plans to install purifying filters. So, at least, claims *Sovietskaya Rossiya*, which had some cutting things to say about the way the local newspaper and plant management extolled the glorious plan – fulfilling achievements of the Azot plant.

If the new Soviet Cultural Fund is to have any role at all as campaigner to protect the national heritage, it will have to take up the cudgels on behalf of Tolstoy's home and its groves of trees, perhaps the greatest shrine of Russian literature.

But if the Fund's spokesmen at press conferences continue with the same shameful prevarications, protestations and lies which devalued Soviet credibility in the past, then it might as well pack up and go home.

In support of that harsh judgement, I cite again the Soviet press, and in particular, the latest issue of *Literaturnaya Gazeta*. One of my favourite Soviet journalists is Olga Chaikovskaya, who launched a battle with the cultural authorities early this year with a brilliant piece of investigative journalism which said that the great Lenin Library was in a state of collapse. She blamed thoughtless tunnelling for the Metro, and spineless administrators.

She now writes that she had never seen a mailbag as big as the one provoked by her article, and quotes several letters who demand that she name each and every blameworthy official. 'If the culprits are not punished and exposed, it means that all our laws on the protection of monuments are a fiction,' thundered one reader.

Olga herself concludes: 'The story of the fate of the Lenin Library gives us a chance to examine the work of "glasnost" (the new official policy of media openness) and to assess just how useful it is.'

That is exactly how I feel about Yasnaya Polyana.

Play power
19 January 1987

The Moscow grapevine is a remarkable phenomenon. About two months ago, people began to ring me up and ask if Andrei Tarkovsky was dead. In fact, he died just after Christmas, in Paris, after two years of voluntary exile. But the rumours were sweeping through Moscow because the cinemas were about to put on a rare season of his films. It must mean he is dead, said the grapevine.

Now there is another rumour that Yuri Lyubimov is on his way back to Moscow, that the Supreme Soviet has decided to return the Soviet citizenship of which they stripped him two years ago. The hope is that he will return to the Taganka Theatre, which he made into the most exciting and provocative in Moscow during the Brezhnev years.

The cultural authorities stopped two vital projects, an attempt to stage the life of the great Taganka actor and poet and balladeer Vladimir Vysotsky, and Lyubimov's own production of *Boris Godunov*. But what he was able to stage has lived on in the memory of Moscow's cultural circles as something that was politically bold as well as artistically outstanding.

They talk of Vysotsky's own performance as Hamlet, which asked what a loyal and decent youth should do when confronted with a rotten kingdom ruled by a corrupt court – a question which resonated dangerously in Brezhnev's Moscow. They talk of the play he made of Trifonov's novel, *The House on the Embankment*, about the informers and the moral price of betrayal during Stalin's purges.

It is broadly assumed in Moscow that Lyubimov was able to survive through the patronage of the then head of the KGB, Yuri Andropov, whose children had once turned up at the Taganka for auditions, hoping to become actors. Lyubimov, who claims he did not know their real identity, turned them down and advised them to look for other careers.

Andropov then summoned Lyubimov to KGB headquarters on Dzerzhinsky Square and thanked him, 'as a father'. His daughter Irina later married a Taganka actor, Alexander Filipov, and this special relationship between the Taganka Theatre and the head of the KGB became widely known in Moscow, not least to the apparatchiks in the ministry of culture who then treated Lyubimov with some delicacy.

Andropov's illness and death in early 1984 robbed Lyubimov of his protector, and after making some critical remarks while producing *Crime and Punishment* in England, he was fired from his Taganka job, expelled from the party, and stripped of his citizenship. One Soviet diplomat at the time had quipped, 'We have the crime, and the punishment will follow.'

The question now in Moscow is what Lyubimov will do if he does return. He has made some political noises about Gorbachev and the cultural thaw in the West. The Taganka has a new, if less spectacular, director, and the mood of cultural Moscow is changing too fast for anyone to keep up.

In Lyubimov's absence, perhaps the most influential director now at work is Oleg Yefremov, who runs the Moscow Arts Theatre. His play, *Silver Wedding*, was the hit of last year, one of the first plays to explore corruption and cynicism among party officials. It is still running, and last month, watching a performance, he noted that while the play had not changed, the audience had.

The lines that had been emphasized, and had excited the audience for their daring last winter, were no longer getting a response.

'The next day, I summoned the cast and we talked about the need to drop the emphasis on the superficial layer of sharp words and gags that sounded new and striking at the première, but have since become common usage,' Yefremov says.

Meanwhile, Slava Spesivtsev is working on a production of Aitmatov's controversial new novel, *Execution Block*, which takes in hashish smokers, drug dealers, and a kind of Russian spiritualism, a search for god. Spesivtsev caused a sensation in the early Seventies with his *Romeo and Juliet*, played by teenagers in a textile factory palace of culture with the actors interspersed with, and often indistinguishable from, the audience.

Then he put on a play about the Russian civil war in a suburban electric train, with most of the passengers not knowing that a performance was taking place.

Spesivtsev has now come out and attacked the whole structure of subsidized theatre, arguing, 'Subsidies support life in what is long dead. The dead should be buried.'

'It would be wonderful if Lyubimov came back,' one of Spesivtsev's actors said to me the other day. 'But I don't think he'll recognize the place.'

A shot for liberty

9 February 1987

This week the Soviet Union is going Pushkin crazy. More than just the great national poet, and the writer whose words form the skeleton for the great Russian operas, he was the man who moulded the Russian language into a great literary style. His life was a romantic epic. He died for love and honour and as a victim of Tsarist autocracy.

Tomorrow, it will be exactly 150 years since Pushkin set off for his duel with d'Anthes. The snow lay so thick that the seconds had to trample it down so that the two men could take the required number of paces and fire. D'Anthes, one of the finest duellists in Europe, fired first and Pushkin fell, mortally wounded, the barrel of his pistol filling with snow.

'I am hurt,' Pushkin said. Then, as d'Anthes began to step forward, the poet called out: 'Do not move. I am still strong enough to fire my shot.' His second brought him another pistol, and leaning forward on his left arm for support, Pushkin fired. He scored a hit, and as d'Anthes fell, Pushkin called out, 'Bravo.'

He spoke too soon, the bullet had gone through the meat of d'Anthes's right arm, which was held across his chest, and then it hit the button on his jacket. D'Anthes survived to return to his native France, to flourish as a financier and to become a senator.

D'Anthes had been a soldier of fortune, a French refugee who had been given a commission in the guards by the Tsar. He had been adopted by the Dutch ambassador at St Petersburg, Baron Heckeren, and the precise relationship between the grand diplomat and the dashing young duellist remains a matter of controversy. But it is known that d'Anthes was being paid a secret pension by the Tsar.

D'Anthes paid court to Pushkin's wife Natalya in the most public and provocative way. Anonymous letters, probably sent by Heckeren, swept through St Petersburg, and one addressed to Pushkin himself appointed him 'official historiographer to the most serene order of cuckolds'. Under the code of honour of the day, Pushkin had little choice but to challenge d'Anthes to a duel. Mikhail Lermontov, in his own verse 'Death of a Poet,' condemned Pushkin's killing as an act of judicial murder, a conspiracy hatched at the Tsarist court to force Pushkin to issue a challenge to one of the best shots in Europe.

The evidence is mixed. The Tsar, who had appointed himself Pushkin's personal censor, had paid off Pushkin's debts and appointed the poet to a humble court pension as a gentleman of the bed-chamber. But that may simply have been a ploy to keep Pushkin, and his popular and beautiful wife, at court. Contemporary gossip suggests that it was the Tsar himself who was really courting Natalya, and that d'Anthes was simply the stalking horse.

But there is no doubt about the political tension between the Tsar and the poet. Pushkin's poems on freedom and the need to abolish serfdom had helped to inspire that generation of well-born liberals who mounted the Decembrist revolt of 1825. His 'Ode to Liberty' of 1817 vowed 'to sing freedom to the world, and crush the vice seated on the throne'. He became a marked man. The police opened his mail, found what they believed to be proof of the crime of atheism, and he was exiled to his family estate at Mikhailovkoye. It was here that he wrote *Eugene Onegin*, and escaped both the Decembrist uprising and the Tsar's repressive revenge.

The Tsar summoned him to court, and Pushkin told him frankly that had he been in St Petersburg, he would have joined his friends in the revolt. It was in this interview that the Tsar appointed himself Pushkin's personal censor, apparently hoping to sway the poet he called 'the most interesting man in Russia' over to his side.

He failed. Pushkin wrote to the Decembrists in their Siberian exile, as Walter Morrison's venerable translation has it:

> Entombed beneath Siberian soil
> Be proudly patient in your pain;
> Your soaring vision and your toil
> Will not have been in vain.

All this gives Pushkin sound anti-Tsarist credentials to be a fit literary hero for the Soviet state.

There is a new film being launched called *The Last Days of Pushkin*, and a special edition of 11 million sets of his complete works in three volumes is being published and is already over-subscribed. At a stately home museum near his Mikhailovskoye estate, a formal costume ball is being held in his honour, and a special state committee has decreed that his death be commemorated around the country.

Mutiny on the boards
23 February 1987

Some of the leading Moscow theatres are in a state close to mutiny as actors challenge the authority of theatre directors in the name of this new mood of democratization and the cultural thaw.

It began with whispers and gossip about the war of nerves that the actors at the Taganka Theatre, where Yuri Lyubimov had made his name, began to wage against his imposed successor, Anotoly Efros.

Efros died in January, but the last months of his life were made a misery as his car tyres were slashed, his fur hat 'disappeared' on winter nights, and childishly rude words were daubed on his fur coat.

At root, it was the fault of the Ministry of Culture bureaucrats. When they fired Lyubimov from his Taganka job, Efros was conscripted to take over. Some of the actors never forgave him – hence the nasty retaliations.

The trouble has now spread to Moscow's prestigious arts theatre, known as Mkhat, and run by Oleg Yefremov. His problem is, in part, financial. Under the new economic reforms, the theatres too are being switched over to the new system of 'khosraschyot', of self-financing and self-accounting. This has not happened yet, and they will continue to need hefty subsidies from the Ministry of Culture, but it does mean that already theatre directors are having to look at costs and the size of their payrolls as never before.

Just as most Soviet newspapers are run by swollen editorial staffs that would arouse the envy of a Fleet Street printer of 1970s vintage, so Soviet theatre companies have such large troops of actors that they could probably stage two different full productions a night and still not have enough room on stage for all the extras.

This will have to change and Yefremov has begun the process in a modest kind of way. He has suggested that his spare actors start performing at a second theatre, along the lines of the Pit at the Barbican or the Theatre Upstairs at the Royal Court.

The actors are up in arms about this, arguing that it will cut back rehearsal times and the production budgets. The whole row has now become public. It was at a curious evening at the Sovremennik Theatre – celebrating its thirtieth anniversary – when some of the recent recruits, who described themselves as 'the refugees from the Taganka' sang a number of satirical and rather vulgar songs on stage attacking Yefros.

It has now got into print, in the latest *Literaturnaya Gazeta*, in an article by one of the most respected Soviet playwrights, Viktor Rozov, a grand man of seventy-four, who managed to survive and prosper through successive Soviet regimes. He claims that 'the welcome democratisation of our life is taking place in the theatre in distorted form'.

The Mkhat Theatre, and Yefremov himself, he warns, are facing 'a catastrophe'. He was the man who used the word 'mutiny' to describe what was going on at the Taganka.

At the Bolshoi, a hesitant new mood of feminism is complaining of 'male imperialism over the choreography'. The argument is that increasingly, the Bolshoi repertoire is dominated by ballets like *Spartacus* and *Icarus* and *Ivan the Terrible*, which favour the male roles. This is partly because of the world-renowned skill of the Moscow male ballet school, but the women claim that the traditions of the art form are being distorted.

Then we have the most politically prominent of Soviet actors, Mikhail Ulyanov, who is a member of the party's Central Committee, claiming that the real problem is that 'we liquidated theatre directors as a class' – staggering words to Russians who recall Stalin's use of that phrase in reference to the Kulaks, the richer peasants who were wiped out to make room for the collective farms.

Ulyanov's point is that the glories of the Soviet stage depended in the past on great directors, like Stanislavky, Meyerhold, and Vakhtangov. The growing authority of the Culture Ministry bureaucrats and the power of the theatre company to influence 'collective' decisions had undermined the creative directors.

And the real dynamite of this, as Rozov points out, is that the theatrical world is just a microcosm of the kind of rows and passions and pent-up frustrations that the economic and political reforms of Gorbachev are bringing to Soviet society as a whole. Only this time, we are seeing them on the open stage.

Soviet take away

9 March 1987

Up on the Sparrow Hills, where the lavish state guest houses enjoy the finest views of Moscow, stands the vast empire of Mosfilm, the Soviet Hollywood. It turns out over forty feature films and dozens of television films a year, employs over 5000 people and exercises a powerful influence over the cultural life of the city.

It is not only the actors, script writers and directors who depend on Mosfilm, not only the obvious symbiosis with the theatres and artists and literary world. Its beauticians and hairdressers and its costumiers ply their trade far beyond the studio walls, more or less legally. But given its resources, and its privileged location in the Soviet capital, its artistic reputation is disappointing.

Some of the better television productions, such as Vassily Livanov's brilliant *Sherlock Holmes* series, are made in the Leningrad studios, where they have a reputation for period drama. The Soviet film the West will hail this year (and a French dubbing is now being prepared for the Cannes festival) is *Pokayaniye* or *Repentance*. A stunning visual achievement in its own right, using allegory and surrealism with a delicacy and precision that goes beyond Fellini, it is a political and historical statement of awesome courage.

But Mosfilm had nothing to do with it. *Pokayaniye* was made in the Georgian film studios. And *Legko Li Bitz Molodim* (*Is It Easy To Be Young?*), the first film to explore specifically the alienation of Soviet youth, from punks to drug addicts to the crippled Afghan veterans, was made in Latvia.

Mosfilm executives have plenty of excuses. As the country's largest studios, they have quotas and plans to fulfil and, living as they do under the sharp eye of the Kremlin, less room to manoeuvre and to experiment. Indeed, in the astonishing flood of reminiscence and settling of old scores that is filling the Soviet press these days, we recently read of the brusque closure of Mosfilm's experimental studios, apparently because they had been too successful.

But they claim at last to be moving, and the other day invited a group of foreign journalists on a short guided tour. It was a fairly depressing experience, because it showed yet again just how difficult it is going to be to adapt the centralized bureaucratic institutions of the Soviet state to Mr Gorbachev's brave new reformist vision.

The plan is for Mosfilm to become self-financing. The problem is how. Under the current system, the state subsidizes each feature film to the tune of an average 400,000 roubles, or £420,000. But this figure does not include the studio overheads, nor the cost of maintaining a vast reserve of cameramen and technicians and so on.

The solution they want to reach is for the Mosfilm studio to become a technical base, renting out its facilities to each successive film project. The Soviet film industry already has its directors. But it must now re-invent the Hollywood producer, the man who puts together the financial package and raises the money that allows the film to be made.

The first problem is that there are no such Hollywood-style producers, and nobody knows how to train them. The second problem is finance. The producers will have to borrow money to make the film, until the money comes back from the cinema audiences. Soviet banks do not work like that.

And frankly, the Soviet cinema distribution system does not work like that either. The manager of a small rural cinema in the Ukraine does not read his film magazines and arrange to rent the latest hit movie. Decisions on what is to be screened, and how often, and where, are taken centrally at the state cinema board, so to set free the Soviet film industry they will have to develop a film finance and venture capital system, find some cinematic entrepreneurs, and transform the distribution system – all at once.

But there are some interesting new projects in the pipeline. The latest fashion seems to be for a kind of upmarket family soap opera, based in the Stalin years. Sergei Kolosov is shooting a television series *Earthly Pleasures* about a family of intellectuals from 1945 to the present, focusing on a scientist who becomes a party administrator and how his need to adapt to a changing party line affects his family.

This theme of the Soviet generation gap is becoming a national obsession, a need to explore the Stalinist past and assess what it did even to those who were spared the gulag. But, as the frustrated executives and directors of Mosfilm are learning, Stalinist institutions live on to frustrate those who would explore the psychological price he made the country pay for his modernizations.

A brush without the law
22 June 1987

They are now more frequent, but a new modern art show in Moscow is still rare enough to stir the bush telegraph and bring the crowds, even without advertisements, posters or stories in the Soviet press.

The Hermitage Group, which has just opened the most remarkable show of all in the ground floor of an apartment block at 100 Profsoyuznaya (or Trade Union Street) is something entirely new. There are some seventy people in the group

– film-makers, artists, sculptors, potters, poets and critics. And for the first time since the 1920s, they are allowed to function and to have premises as an independent art collective, without sheltering under the protective wing of a trade union or party group.

They are currently battling for the right to earn some legal money by charging admission for their exhibitions and selling the paintings from the walls. But this kind of venture is so new that there are no rules, and the local council which gave them the premises has no idea who can give permission to collect money from the public.

So, for the moment, entry is free. On the right is the alternative fashion – dresses in slashed black leather that look more gladiator than S and M. Straight ahead is the Buttermilk Statement, a vast pillar of the waxed-paper packaging that wraps 'kefir', or Soviet buttermilk. Some solidified stuff stands alongside in glass laboratory jars.

To the left is a corridor with what looks like school blazers and jackets and raincoats hanging limply on the wall. Then you realize that they are carved from wood and painted. At the end of the corridor is another large room with a strip cartoon that starts on the ceiling and runs along about fifty yards of floor space and tells the history of Soviet art.

Stalin's jackboot and his pipe make a guest appearance, along with Krushchev calling modern art 'dogshit' and the bulldozers that cleared away an open-air art exhibition in the Seventies. It finishes with the coming of consumer goodies, the Soviet artist painting in Western jeans while the stereo tape deck blares out music, rock concerts take place in the Manezh exhibition hall, and the amateur artists hang out their paintings amid the birch trees in Bitza Park.

'It is about the death of heroism,' said a Russian friend, and I suppose she is right.

From the ceiling hangs a vast cardboard cylinder, painted white. As your eye follows the long phallic shape, it becomes unmistakably a rocket, one of the modern Soviet icons from the Red Square parades.

The walls are a riot of collages and paintings and strange, unsettling shapes that would hardly raise an eyebrow in the West but which here retain their shock value.

It is hard to be sure of any single trend in Moscow these days, with Gorbachev taking two steps forward and the party edging one step back. This bold new experiment in un-supervised art was allowed to take place just a few days after Kantor, Dibsky and Boris Markovnikov, three of the most talented young artists in the city, were turned down for membership of the Artists' Union by the neanderthals. This kind of rejection is a serious matter. Without union member-ship, you have no right to a workshop, to the specialist stores of paints and brushes and canvases, and only a shadowy right to earn a living as an artist.

There is some good news. For the first time that anyone can remember, there is a Western artist included in the Hermitage Group, and showing four paintings.

Mathew Cullerne-Bown is in Moscow, attached to the Strogonov Art Institute, the first artist to come and work on a British Council fellowship. 'It mainly trains people to be social realist painters, so I began looking around, meeting other artists and found myself with this lot,' he said, looking politely at the Buttermilk Statement.

'Some people say my paintings are the only really Soviet works in the exhibition.'

They are certainly different, a Westerner responding to the novelty of the Soviet symbols of cosmonauts' helmets and building workers' hard hats, blending them into a three-dimensional loose grid inspired by the Moscow Metro map.

This offering of British art may well be seen by more Muscovites than the touring Royal Ballet, because the Her-mitage Group has been given a peach of a location. Just outside the exhibition is one of the most popular spots in Moscow, a large notice board advertising flat swaps.

Dead letters

9 November 1987

For some months now, the phrase 'cultural necrophilia' has haunted Russia's literary world. Gorbachev's cultural thaw means that Moscow has become the city of the living dead, feeding on the stored-up fat of nearly seventy years of banned books and forbidden authors. At times, it is like living in a time-warp.

The poets Yevgeny Yevtushenko and Andrei Vosnesensky have been in the forefront of the campaign for the thaw, just as they were in Krushchev's time twenty-five years ago, and the familiar battle has been raging over whether at last to publish Boris Pasternak's famous novel *Dr Zhivago* just as it raged then.

This time the good guys have won, and Pasternak's Nobel-prize-winning account of the way the revolution killed off, perverted and overwhelmed the old Russian intelligentsia is to be published in February.

The cult of the past dominates Soviet intellectuals today. Everyone is flocking to the exhibition of some 300 of Marc Chagall's paintings, a posthumous affair to celebrate the 100th birthday of an artist banned since he decamped from the Soviet Union in disgust back in 1922.

In the theatre, the hit play of the season was Nikolai Erdman's *Suicides*, banned since 1930. The first sign of the thaw in the film world was the decision of the new secretary of the film union, Elem Klimov, (whose own films spent years gathering dust on the censor's shelf) to establish a commission to review all the films banned in the past.

Soviet literary life revolves around the thick journals like *Novy Mir* where 'new' novels and poems first appear, and for the past year they have been dominated by the literary energy of the old days. The great poem has been Akhmatova's 'Requiem', the lament which compares the mothers of Stalin's purge victims to Mary at the crucifixion. This was matched by the belated publication of the poems of her first husband, Nikolai Gumilyov, banned since he was shot as a counter-revolutionary back in 1921. The great novel has been Rybakov's *Children of the Arbat,* about the murder of Kirov which began Stalin's purges, and written thirty years ago.

These events have caught the imagination of the West because they mark the great gap that has been torn in the wall that the Communist Party and its censors had erected around the national memory. Stalin's victims, and his crimes, have emerged into the public domain, and the sense of liberation and long-overdue honesty that all this represents is the most powerful possible symbol of the new era of Gorbachev.

And yet, not all of this is healthy. I know of no significant or even interesting Russian writer of our own day who is under thirty years old. The ones under forty can be counted on the fingers of one hand. The standard-bearers of the new cultural thaw are a group of brave editors, all into their fifties and sixties, who were inspired by the Krushchev thaw, dismayed by the grim philistinism of Brezhnev's day, and who are now determined to print the forbidden fruit of the past while they can. There is a window of opportunism of which they are taking advantage in the ever-haunting fear that the mood or the man in the Kremlin might change, and the window be slammed shut once more. But this great flood of the cultural past is in danger of washing out everything else.

That phrase 'cultural necrophilia' first became current among a group of contemporary writers who saw their own work piling up on the editors' desks because there was less and less room to print it. In a country where newsprint is still rationed, the literary boom for an old writer means less paper available to publish the new.

This has had the mundane but important effect of hitting a lot of writers in their pockets. Some of the overpaid and overprinted hacks of Brezhnev's day deserve it, but others do not, and their grievances are starting to build up an ominous kind of coalition which suspects that all this digging up and feeding off the carcass of the past is going rather too far.

Perhaps the most alarming figure of this type, because he is a fine novelist who explored difficult and unpredictable themes, is Yuri Bondarev. He began by writing best-sellers about World War Two like *Battalions Request Covering Fire,* and then established his anti-Stalinist credentials in Krushchev's time with *Silence,* about a war veteran caught up in Stalin's terror.

Later books like *The Shores* explored the love-hate relationship between Russians and Germans.

At this year's meeting of the Russian Writers' Union, Bondarev used a powerful wartime metaphor to rally the old guard. 'We have had our June of 1941,' he said, as if comparing the cultural thaw to Hitler's invasion, 'but one day we shall have our Stalingrad,' he added grimly.

4
Not So High Arts

Much of the fun I had in Moscow, and many of the friends I made, came from the kind of artistic world that has nothing to do with the Bolshoi ballet and grand opera. Except that it was these modern artists and rock musicians and fashion designers and experimental poets and film-makers who made Moscow such an exciting place to be in the first years of Gorbachev.

We now look back at Berlin in the Weimar years before Hitler, or at Paris in the *belle époque* or even Swinging London of the 1960s as distinct and quite special cultural moments, when social change and political tension and artistic creativity and daring all combined into a heady, magical cocktail of a period. Under the impact of Gorbachev's cultural thaw, Moscow was like that. And it was all the more thrilling and poignant because there had never been anything quite like it in living memory. All-night cinemas, a jazz club where they played till dawn, rock concerts in the parks and avant-garde fashion shows in ruined churches, experimental theatres in gloomy basements, new literary magazines being published without anyone's permission – Moscow was suddenly bubbling with long-suppressed excitements and possibilities.

And it was the emergence of this kind of counter-culture, this proof that there was life after the Bolshoi, that provided the best guarantee that the Gorbachev reforms were real. It was not simply that the long-forbidden was being allowed to flourish. It also pointed to the vast amount of creative and dangerous energy that had been building up during the long stagnation of the Brezhnev years. When I first arrived in Moscow, with the elderly invalid Konstantin Chernenko (Who?) nominally in power, I quickly began to sense that in spite of the moribund immobility at the top, this was a society that was pregnant with change. And even while *Pravda* was silent, the cultural fringe was the place to gather clues about the way that change might develop. It was also the most enjoyable milieu in Moscow.

Rambo in red

23 June 1986

At the video salon on the Arbat pedestrian precinct in central Moscow, the latest hot property is Russia's own Rambo movie. Under the title *Lonely Journey* you get the Soviet Union's own version of the SAS, the Spetznatz naval commandos, wiping out hordes of wicked Americans and saving the world in the process.

A film classic it is not, but the locations are tropically wonderful, the camera work fine, the girls look terrific in bikinis and the special effects are well up to Hollywood standards. The jugulars really spout blood as the throwing knives sink in, and the last few moments of the flight of the anti-ship missile and the subsequent explosion are lavishly done.

The plot is fairly simple, as these things go. The CIA is planning to blow up a luxury cruise liner and blame it on the Russians. Behind the CIA is a group of golf-loving fat cats who represent the military–industrial complex. They want a new superpower crisis that will be good for profits.

In a magnificently louche tropical night club we meet Hessel, the maddest man in the CIA, whose drinking bouts are interspersed with flashbacks to atrocities in Vietnam.

Armed with all the latest technology, Hessel arranges the missile strike on the cruise ship. But something goes wrong. The missile hits instead a private sailing yacht, being sailed happily round the world by a slightly hippy young American couple. They are blown into the water, but quickly set themselves up on a desert island with all the usual accoutrements of castaways, luxury tents, short-wave radios, Kalashni-kov rifles – that sort of thing.

The frustrated Hessel does not want any surviving witnesses to his schemes, and while the CIA officially disavows him, Hessel sets up an assassination team against the American castaways, who fly in on hang-gliders to ambush the tent.

But meantime, the good guys have woken up. On the sunny deck of a Soviet naval ship, a group of marine Spetznatz are going through their friendly unarmed combat practice, and talking of old folks at home and the fun of hunting mushrooms in the forests.

The ship's captain has monitored the flight of the missile, learned of the CIA's plan, and assigns the nostalgic Spetznatz boys to frustrate it. Just as any American hit-team of this type contains the token negro and token Spanish American, this one contains the token central Asian and a young lad from Siberia who is too young to die.

The mayhem begins. The Americans in their tent are just getting amorous when the hang-glider assassins cut their way through the canvas, kill the girl, and are killed in turn by her vengeful husband. He starts to hunt down the CIA killers, the Russians arrive to help, and the young American joins the good guys.

This is important. The fact that the Russian commandos cheerfully welcome this lethal hippy into their ranks is what makes this movie ideologically correct, proving that Moscow is not against the American people, but only against the bad guys.

Back in his submarine command post, Hessel thinks this is the right time to start World War Three. But, having wiped out the CIA assassins, the Russians and our hippy hero go after Hessel. They grenade and shoot and punch their way into the control room just as Hessel's crazed finger is poised over the button.

And inevitably the Spetznatz leader dies at the moment of triumph, shot in the back by the cowardly villain.

What makes *Lonely Journey* stand out from the usual Soviet thriller movie is the lavishness of its budget, spent on the foreign locations and the expensive sets – all doomed to be blown up. But the Soviet movie-goer – and the average Soviet citizen goes to the cinema 14 times a year – gets the same kind of regular diet of these 'patriotic' films that we do.

There was *Flight 222* set in an Aeroflot jet at New York airport where the Americans try in vain to persuade a loyal Soviet woman to stay in the West with her defected husband.

There was the hit TV series *Tass is authorised to state . . .* about the attempts by the CIA to destabilize a small African country, and the heroic efforts of the KGB to keep the place safe for peace and socialism.

There is something international about these stereo-typed images we keep churning out about each other. Something depressing about the way that our Rambo and their Spetznatz depend upon the same hardware of machine pistol and grenade. Patriotic violence is as American as cherry pie, as Russian as borscht, or as British as the Falkland Islands.

But there was one interesting thing about the video of *Lonely Journey* that we hired overnight from the Arbat salon for a rouble. The video tape itself was made in Japan.

Park in chains

5 January 1987

About two years ago, not long after starting to live in Moscow, we were taken along to Bitza Park, where the informal open-air art gallery had just begun to operate. Bitza is way out in the southern suburbs, where the constant building of high-rise apartments starts to give way to open country, and untamed enough for the jogger to be attacked by the packs of wild dogs, abandoned by their owners, who are becoming an urban menace.

Bitza is more interesting than most of the Moscow parks because of its hills, steep enough to make the cross-country skiing just a little hazardous, and because it feels like real countryside.

But over the past two years, the artists have become the real attraction. At first, there were intermittent problems with the police, but the artists kept coming back, propping their works against tree trunks, on the park benches, or in open suitcases, ready for a quick getaway.

Some of the themes were slightly provocative – mock icons and crucifixion scenes, but mainly Bitza was a place where Sunday painters could sell their clumsy landscapes and little sketches of country churches.

Then the hippies started to come, with their hand-carved Buddhas and astrological signs, their home-made jewellery and bead necklaces. And soon after came the artistic wide boys, who normally sell their glossy acrylic sunsets from the doorways outside the state art salons.

Last winter, it all made for a pleasant Sunday. We could take the children sledging, and then ski the trails through the park to the children's village of miniature wooden houses. And when the children got cold, the painters would usually have a small fire going behind the park benches, where they could stand and get warm.

But the customers came in ever greater numbers. You could no longer ski from one painter to the next, but shuffled along in a crowd. More and more painters began to arrive, and the long stretch of pathway had become a Moscow version of London's Bayswater Road – a long alley of overpriced kitsch.

Last summer it was no longer a very pleasant place to visit. Then came the Gorbachev reforms, encouraging co-operatives and private enterprise, and on the face of it, removing any lingering doubts about the legality of the Bitza Park artists.

But it does not seem to have worked out quite so easily. The borough which includes Bitza Park is called Sevastopolski Raion, and they have come up with a depressing way of interpreting the new co-op structure.

They have said that every artist who wants to join the Bitza Park co-op must pay 10 roubles a month – a day's average pay for a Moscow worker – and every customer who wants to buy a painting must also pay 30 kopeks to the local borough. A customer must also show his identity documents to the official who will take charge of the paperwork.

The money thus raised will go to pay for the paperwork, and also for the high wire fences that the borough proposes to erect around the area which will be designated the official private art sale area.

So the whole point of Bitza will be lost. We will no longer be able to stroll along the rows of paintings as part of a day out in the open air. We will have to queue outside the fenced-off compound, pay our 30 kopeks to get inside, and then look at the pictures. Half the fun of the place used to be the haggling over prices, but I cannot see there being much bargaining in such a structured atmosphere with borough officialdom breathing down one's neck.

It is all rather depressing, and bodes ill for the way the Gorbachev reforms on private enterprise and co-ops will work out in practice. The Soviet Union is a country where bureaucracy is as natural as breathing. But if open-air art sales are to require fences, identity cards, and full-time officials, Mr Gorbachev's hesitant foray into free enterprise is doomed before it begins.

In the centre of Moscow, near the Taganka Theatre, is the pet market, which has been functioning happily enough for years under another borough's administration. There, the would-be vendors hire a stall for the day to sell their puppies or pet food, their hand-made aquariums, and dog collars. It costs a rouble for the day, and although there is a wire fence, there is nobody to check your papers. I hope there are no plans to 'liberate' the pet market into the new co-op structure.

Loosing their chains
2 February 1987

The conference hall at Mgimo, the Moscow State Institute for International Relations, had never seen anything like it. Mgimo has been described as a Soviet Eton, the Foreign Ministry's diplomatic college where bright and usually well-connected young Soviets are trained for careers as diplomats, foreign correspondents, and the other plum jobs which carry the cherished prospect of overseas travel.

Certainly its conference hall is the plushest auditorium I have seen in the Soviet Union. Its seats were armchairs, upholstered in a tasteful royal blue, the backs so high that you could rest your head and take a discreet nap.

But there was no sleeping on the night that the hall presented an evening of Soviet heavy metal rock music. The well-equipped sound and light systems were tested to the limits as the bands swung their chains and their waist-length hair and wielded their imported electric guitars like so many axes.

The place was packed, with standing room only. But only a tiny knot of forty or so real *metallisti* gathered by the front of the stage to dance and shoot out their arms in the rhythmic heavy metal salutes. The bulk of the crowd were rather staid and well-dressed, clean-cut young people. The concert had been organized by the adventurous local *Komsomol*, or party youth organization, of the Gagarin borough of southern Moscow.

It had not been billed as a concert. My ticket said: 'We invite you to the first meeting of the rock club, dealing with the problems of heavy metal.'

After the first session, by a terribly amateurish band called Black Coffee, the serious discussion began. There were microphones for everyone who wanted to speak, and a lively debate soon got under way. One well-dressed young lad in a polo neck began by saying it was rubbish, and the *metallisti* leapt to their band's defence.

'The kids played good,' said one with metal-studded armbands. Then the mike was taken by a young man dressed from head to foot in black leather, with an ironmongery of chains and crosses festooned around his neck, earrings shaped like big silver crosses, and thick black hair halfway down his back.

A doctor at a local clinic is one of the most famous of the Moscow *metallisti* fans, the most manic dancer, so well-known to the bands that they give him a mike to sing along with all their songs that he knows by heart. When heavy metal was so popular among Soviet youth, he wanted to know, why did Melodiya, the state recording company, not release it on disc?

A man then stood up, introduced himself as the head of advertising at Melodiya, and said that some records had already been released. He cited an album by the next band on the programme, a powerful and highly professional Estonian group called Gunnar Graps. If Black Coffee came up with some good songs, he would be happy to hear them, he said.

The impact of this response was blunted when another young *metallist* took the mike to say he could hardly believe that Melodiya executives really existed. And now he was seeing one with his own eyes. He put down the mike, trotted up to the Melodiya man, and engaged him in spirited conversation.

Then one of the producers of the lively TV programme *Up to 16 and Older* took the floor, and got the kind of response a producer of *Spitting Image* might get at a similar event in Britain. One of the most sprightly examples of the new glasnost on Soviet TV, it features outspoken interviews with young rock fans, irreverent humour and a freewheeling style.

He promised a new late-night TV programme for young people, to include clips of Western video, reports from foreign correspondents on Western youth and their music, and said that heavy metal was a part of the youth scene that simply should not be ignored.

The openness had its limits. The only other Western correspondent who wangled an invitation, for CBS TV News, was turned away with his camera at the door, on Foreign Ministry orders. A pity. When Moscow's top-heavy metal group Ariya came on, with their dry-ice smoke and heavy make-up, it was a marvellous show, rather like being at an Iron Maiden or Judas Priest concert back in the 1970s. Even the striped-pant costumes and chain dog-collars were identical.

But then their music was well-tailored to a Mgimo concert. Their best song was 'Not for us', about how Soviet youth did not want to play Western-style military video-games. We may be heavy metal, went the message – but no aggro, please, we're Russian.

Red taped stars

16 March 1987

Ever since I first heard them, I knew that any future historian of the West in the 1960s would have to reckon with the lyrics to the song 'My Generation', by the Who.

I have that feeling again about the Soviet Union in the 1980s, after listening with some care to songs by the two leading bands for Soviet kids today.

I doubt whether either of them has yet been heard of in the West, but Televisor of Leningrad and Zvuki Mu of Moscow are by a mile the most important bands now working in the Soviet Union. I'm not sure 'working' is the right word. Even with the new cultural thaw, they have barely emerged from underground status.

Melodiya, the state recording monopoly, does not issue their records, and you will not hear them on Soviet radio or television. Their popularity rests on live performance and on the ubiquitous bootleg tapes made at their concerts.

For the last three months, we had not heard much of Televisor. They were banned from their main venue, the Leningrad Rock Club, after culture officials listened carefully to their lyrics.

'Outta control, outta control, we all have to get, outta control,' which is becoming a kind of underground youth anthem, was less than popular in official circles.

Then there was the song about the neanderthals in the Ministry of Culture, which has the stirring chorus:

> Nothing will change
> and no one will change
> no way and no how
> while these stiffs remain in power.

And there is the breakdance song, about the cultural thaw:

> OK – so they let us break-dance
> OK – so we can be happy sometimes.

> But still standing behind the column is
> the man in the thin tie with cement in his eyes.

So far, there have been no problems for Zvuki Mu, a rock-band which features an oboe among the usual guitars and drums, and a lead singer whose stage performance has elevated St Vitus's Dance into an art form.

They first became known with a song about kids hating to go to school, that sang of 'too much football and the teachers' dead faces' and which finished on the chorus that every Moscow schoolkid seems to know: 'Daddy, you'd better buy me a Walkman.'

But the other night – at a hall in the southern suburbs where I trailed out to see them – they sang a number called 'Soyuzpechat', which is the word used for the state newspaper distribution system. Mr Gorbachev's policy of glasnost, or openness in the Soviet press, has not left them much impressed:

> In the mornings, when I finally go home,
> Is when I want what I can never get.
> It was the fresh printed papers
> That taught me to dream.
> It was the Soyuzpechat
> That taught us how to wait
> When you pass me by
> Don't make that kind of face
> As if you couldn't give a spit
> What the papers and this country say about us.
> And remember, the money we all make is false money.
> Counterfeit paper – Soyuzpechat.

One of the underground rock 'fanzies', or fan magazines, which ran a double-column review of 1986 and preview of 1987, named Zvuki Mu as the band of 1986 and Televisor the band of 1987. It also gave listings for 'Dread of the Year,' with radio-activity in 1986 and Aids in 1987. It listed 'legislation of rock' as the achievement of the year in 1986, and 'glasnost' as anti-climax of the year.

'Nostalgia of the Year' was cheap wine for 1986 and underground rock concerts for 1987. That may prove premature after Televisor's trouble. And I have my fears for Zvuki Mu's satirical song about perestroika:

> They used to say we had to strike proudly forward.
> Now they say we have to jump proudly forward.
> But we have to turn round first
> And they never taught us to turn round.

Culture shock

6 April 1987

The theme of this year's Edinburgh Festival is the celebration of Soviet art, and the Bolshoi orchestra and the Gorky Theatre from Leningrad, and the Shostakovich quartet, and other members of the great and good of Soviet high arts are to appear.

Sadly, I know little of the way the fringe of the Edinburgh Festival is organized, but if anyone has some spare halls and wants to celebrate the future of Soviet arts rather than the grand and distinguished past, let me make some suggestions.

We had better begin with the surprising fact that Moscow these days has become one of the most exciting cultural cities on earth, bubbling with ideas and projects and a creativity too long held down. There are poetry readings and experimental theatre studios, and groups who call themselves constructivist and situationist art movements, and multimedia experiments happening all over the place.

Leaving aside alternative comedy, which has yet to reach the level of Alexei Sayle's historic attack on 'Guardian readers who knit their own yogurt', I would start out with some rather good films. There is a brilliant Latvian documentary on youth alienation called Is It Easy to be Young? – which intersperses disillusioned and embittered Afghan veterans with Soviet punks and druggies. That is one reminder that the world is a small place, and so is my next suggestion,

Rollan Sergienko's shattering new documentary called *Tolling Bell of Chernobyl*.

Then there is theatre. The experimental and largely amateur group who have been playing in a vast black-painted basement and call themselves Studio-Theatre of the South-West, are a drama group of staggering talent and invention. They staged the most memorable *Hamlet* I have ever seen, and their new production of Vonnegut's *Tell Me that You Love Wanda Jean* is the talk of Moscow. Forget any language barrier, their performance of a jazz musical set in a 1920s hotel-whorehouse called *Three Top Hats* would succeed anywhere.

Then there are the brand-new art movements, like Attention Experiment, which is producing an exhibition-cum-happening-cum-performance at the splendidly-named Palace of Culture of the Hammer and Sickle factory.

Another group calling themselves the Avantgardists are trying to stage a similar event at a municipal exhibition hall near the Zil auto factory in eastern Moscow, a throwing together of art and music and declamation and disputation whose very exuberance is its main justification.

The local party officials were reeling with shock as the exhibition was set up on Saturday, stunned by the caricatures of Colonel Gaddafi and Pol Pot, the satirical daubings of stinking fish and champagne glasses on a poster that announced 'the party cadres will decide everything', and the crude symbolism of a series of paintings about the decadence and rot of the Roman Empire.

It will be an interesting test of the limits of the new cultural freedom to see if the show actually opens today as scheduled.

The good and the bad and the plain experimental are all jostling and thriving together as people grow in confidence and daring. But I think there would be few doubts about the budding genius of a young Estonian musician, Erki Sven Tturi, who is writing modern classical music of astonishing power.

The son of a preacher, and born on a remote Baltic island, he combined study in a music conservatory with weekends playing for a local rock-jazz group who had been much influenced by Mike Oldfield. He then began arranging ancient folk music for a group of Baltic musicians who were restoring old instruments to re-create an authentic sound, before embarking on his own music, from string quartets to oratorios.

Finally, there ought to be a Soviet rock concert of the groups that the state concert monopoly has traditionally shunned. A chum of mine, John Burrows, who runs the Capital music festival in London came to Moscow recently to find some Soviet bands for his show. I took him to hear Zvuki Mu, which is probably the most exciting and innovative of the groups. 'Not for my kind of mass market festival, but they'd do well at the Edinburgh fringe,' said John. So I pass on his expert advice.

The Lithuanian band, Antis, hardly ever comes to Moscow, but I think they might have appealed to him more. They do a marvellous stage show based around their lead singer, who stands nearly 7 ft tall and looks like Count Dracula on crack. And if the Leningrad band Televisor have sorted out the problems of their provocative lyrics with the Ministry of Culture, they ought to be there too. Indeed, the problem these days in drawing up lists of the most exciting events in Moscow is deciding what to leave out.

Artists, but not on paper
4 May 1987

This is a sad story, and one that does not bode well for glasnost, for freedom in the arts, nor for the bureaucratic support and initiative that will be required to follow through the Gorbachev reforms.

This year has seen the tenth anniversary of a group of Moscow artists who call themselves simply The Twenty. They first came to prominence early in the 1970s when they were among a much larger group of avant-garde painters who mounted an unofficial exhibition in Moscow's Ismailovo

Park, and whose works were bulldozed away in one of the most ridiculous and philistine displays of KGB arrogance.

The outcry in the West and among Soviet artistic circles, was such that a compromise was eventually reached. The Twenty were not allowed into the Artists' Union, which would have given them automatic rights to separate workshops, to paint and brushes and canvases, to subsidized annual holidays and a guaranteed income, and papers that showed they were in gainful employment. Indeed, because of the bureaucratic rigidities of the Artists' Union, they did not want that.

But they were found a kind of semi-status attached to the Guild of Illustrators, and given an annual exhibition in the cramped basement of a trade union building. And every year their exhibition is one of the best attended in Moscow, with more than 80,000 people paying last year for admission.

This year is just as crowded, and their themes have not changed very much. Sergei Simakov is still painting vast canvases of a passionate religious nationalism. His latest is a lovingly detailed battle painting of a siege of an Orthodox monastery, the priests holding up icons as the heroic Russians leap out to smite the Tartar invaders.

Vladislav Provotorov would have found fame and fortune in the West designing the sleeves for rock albums and the cover of science fiction books. He paints nightmarish scenes and technical fantasies with awesome precision. This year, his Trojan Horse, being hauled through a crumbling fortress wall and spilling ghastly corpses while clouds boil in a sullen sky, is a formidable piece of work.

Vitaly Linitsky and his wife Vasilissa combine the two forms, with religious themes that are suffused with light, crosses like giant searchlights, and ghostly beams coming from Heaven to illuminate humble Russian Orthodox churches below.

The rumbustious Dmitri Gordeyev presents wonderfully bucolic scenes of Muscovites at their summer beaches, and slightly grotesque nudes that make you think of Lucian Freud in a joyful mood. Igor Snegur, one of the oldest members of the group, and one who is entitled to his own workshop as a member in good standing of the Union of Journalists, is still producing his tightly-controlled pastel abstracts.

The point is that this kind of work no longer shocks. You can see the religious–nationalist themes at the exhibitions of Glazunov, the much-abused court painter of the Brezhnev regime, or at the open-air market in Bitza Park any weekend.

And yet the Soviet bureaucracy still refuses to accept them as artists. In a land where it remains vital to possess the proper documents that attest your right to exist, to reside in Moscow and to work, they have no such papers. They are intermittently harassed and threatened with prosecution under the regulation which outlaws 'parasitism' and makes a job obligatory. They have no right to paints, brushes or canvases, but have to queue with the amateur painters at the ill-stocked public shops.

'Times are harder now, and I am getting worried about going hungry,' says Vladimir Petrov-Gladkii. 'In the West, everyone seems to assume that Gorbachev has liberalized everything, and the foreign galleries and collections that once supported us are looking elsewhere. New export taxes make it prohibitive for foreigners to buy our paintings, and now the new checks on incomes make it harder for Russians to buy our work.'

Not all of the works of The Twenty are to my taste, and some of my other artist friends mock them slightly as 'valuta-painters', who grew accustomed to selling to transient Western diplomats and businessmen looking for something authentically Russian that was also rather daring. But there is no doubting their dedication, nor the range of their talents.

A month ago, the editor of *Ogonyok*, now one of the most outspoken examples of glasnost and innovation in the Soviet media, invited The Twenty to a discussion of their problems and to prepare a major feature on them and their work. Somehow, it never appeared.

Soviet Hammer but no Sickle
29 June 1987

This last weekend, Moscow held its first art auction for seventy years. The last such event, I am told, took place in 1916 when paintings from the collections of the Tsar and his court were auctioned for the war effort. In a way, we have the Kremlin's first lady, Raisa Gorbachev, to thank for this return to marketing normality. She is the key patron of the new Soviet cultural fund, under whose auspices the event was arranged. The fund managed to acquire permanent premises and exhibition space at 15 Karl Marx Street, which also happens to be the old palace of the Golitzyn family, on a fine old street which contains the old Uspensky Mansion and several other grand homes from the old days.

The street used to be called Old Seal, and just opposite the splendidly restored Golitzyn Palace is the sadly decrepit Church of Nicholas the Martyr.

It was poignant to sit in the auction hall and glance out of the window at the weeds and small trees growing from the ledges around its bell-tower. But the skills and enthusiasms of Arseny Lobanov soon changed my mood. He is the Soviet Union's only professional auctioneer, the chap who runs the twice-yearly auctions for Western buyers, and the sales of yearling horseflesh. The Russians breed good horses, and among the many languages in which Arseny can count is Arabic.

But furs and horseflesh have that special licence which is enjoyed by those Soviet goods which are sold for hard currency. Modern art has, so far, not been among them. Glasnost and Raisa and the cultural fund have combined to change all that. When the exhibition of 'Young Moscow artists' was first opened for viewing ten days ago, I was struck to see Comrade Alexander Nikolaev, the ambitious young first secretary of the Party Committee for Bauman Borough, make one of the formal speeches. It then turned out he was chairman of the newly-formed local branch of the friends of the cultural fund.

Even two years ago, a rising young star of the Moscow Party machine would not have been seen dead within miles of a modern art show. But now what was once frowned upon is all the rage. When Raisa came along for her own private viewing, she enthused over the aggressive and highly-coloured canvases of a young chum of mine, Yevgeny Dubskii. He has already had a couple of exhibitions in France and Germany, and is one of the bright young hopes of Soviet art.

Because of Raisa's approval, he was asked to sit in an aisle seat, perfectly positioned for the TV cameras. But when his paintings came up to auction, one oil with a reserve price of 1000 roubles and two water colours at 250 roubles, there were no bidders. Indeed, there were no bids for thirty of the fifty-six paintings that were auctioned on the first day. The highest price that was paid was 550 roubles for a rather ordinary urban landscape with a reserve price of 375 roubles. The lady who was bidding had not quite understood the rules, understandably after so many years of no auctions, and began bidding against herself.

The golden-tongued Arseny turned to her, his bronzed dark glasses glinting in the TV lights, and said, 'The bid is yours, madame, at 550 roubles.'

'Six hundred,' she shouted decisively.

'No dear,' he explained, 'we'll save your old man some money.' And he slammed down his hammer. Sold.

The most popular items were four charming primitives, painted on wooden bread boards. There was a scene inside an old Siberian log cabin, a couple making love on top of the stove while grandpa brews up some moonshine vodka and granny bakes bread in the oven. There was another set inside a tailor's shop. With reserve prices of 120 to 180 roubles, they attracted furious bidding, up to 300 roubles, as the first lucky buyer bid and bid to acquire the set.

Most of the oil paintings, by the best-known young artists like Maxim Kantor, were called in after attracting no bids at all. I got into a tussle with an art critic from one of the Soviet papers and a well-heeled Eastern European diplomat for a crude but intriguing painting of evidently drunken fishermen, but I dropped out and the bids finally soared to 500 roubles. I finally picked up a sub-Magritte surrealist and funny painting at its reserve price of 150 roubles.

'It was a great success, and we will now go on to hold more such auctions, of photographs and stage designs,' said the organizer, Lev Rubinsky. 'I'm not depressed that so many went unsold. That happens in the West too, but as for our pricing policy, we may have to think again.'

Poets rock the boat
13 July 1987

As we stepped aboard the good ship *Moscow River Boat 14*, the constructivist poet Dmitri Aleksandrich handed each of us a different short poem. Mine read: 'Citizen, you have often had the self-same thought before, only better.'

The small stars and stripes flag woven into Dmitri's beard waggled in time with his grin. On the quayside, four young men in black shirts stood to attention as a hand-wound and ancient gramophone played 'Arrivederci, Roma'.

As our boat, bearing the members and guests of the Avantgardisti cultural club pulled away into the Moscow River, the young men unfolded a banner which read, 'Come back to your senses.'

If the suspicious old dinosaurs who still run so much of Soviet cultural life had known about this boat trip and picnic in advance, one well-placed limpet mine or torpedo would probably have wiped out Soviet artistic life for the next 40 years.

Alexei Parshikov, the most striking of the new generation of Soviet poets, lounged at the ship's rail, looking disconcertingly like the famous portrait of Pushkin, and debated whether rationalism had been a nineteenth-century phenomenon in Russia, or whether the country had really shared in the European rationalism of the eighteenth century. His wife Olga is exceedingly beautiful, the brightest modern art critic in Moscow, and a focus of creative energy that fuels the new experimental video club, the new Avantgardisti group and half the cultural energy in the country.

She was making a film of the boat outing, suspecting with her usual optimism that this would be a historic day in the development of Russian culture, while cursing the incompetence of the Soviet economic system which had caused another nationwide shortage of film stock. Five productions being shot at the Mosfilm studios are currently stood down because of lack of film. Olga had characteristically managed to acquire a video camera instead. Art will find a way.

The last man to jump aboard as we pulled away was Africa, an ex-punk young musician from Leningrad. His pink hair and conviction that reinforced concrete is an indispensable component of modern music will be recalled by anyone who saw the BBC television series *Comrades*.

Downstairs, the young artists who have formed a comic rock group, with a punning name that can be translated as Central Russian Hills or Average Russian Attitudes, were hammering out their best-known song. Its chorus goes:

> Mummy, you told me daddy was just a black man.
> You didn't tell me he was an American spy.

Our medium-sized river steamer passed a much larger and grander boat with the proud name *October Revolution*. That provoked many Gorbachev-era jokes about the revolution being left far behind.

Grisha Brushkin came by for a chat. He is the young artist whose *Fundamental Lexicon* was one of the stars of the seminal modern art exhibition back in February, the event that signalled the reality and the possibilities of the Gorbachev cultural thaw. The 128 miniatures that made up the painting, a subtly devastating satire of the iconography of the Soviet state through an exaggerated portrayal of its own favourite symbols and self-images, was bought by the Czech film director Milos Forman. But Grisha was worried. 'It would be terrible if modern Soviet art was simply seen in the West as something exotic, like African masks, just another new fashion,' he grumbled. 'We exist on our own terms. We have a right to be judged on the world's terms, to learn, to teach and contribute.'

A passing young film critic applauded solemnly. He was wearing only underpants, on which the gold star of a hero of the Soviet Union was pinned, and he handed out lottery tickets. The prizes were modern paintings by the Avantgardisti group. Curious, since he is part of the other significant modern art group of Moscow, known as The Hermitage, and I suspect a Montague–Capulet style of cultural rivalry may be in the offing.

We reached the picnic spot, swam and rented rowing boats, ate and drank and talked the hot summer's day away as the river police launches circled offshore like worried midges.

At 7 p.m., the boat's siren summoned us back, and Dmitri had unfurled a vast banner on the boat deck that read, 'Who are you with, renaissance man?' The twilight slowly darkened over the Bay of Joys as the band roared into 'Born in the USSR'.

5
Lifestyles

It can be a frustrating business, being a Moscow correspondent. We send back to the West our news reports, our abstruse analyses of Kremlinology, our reviews of cultural life and our descriptions of ordinary life. We try to cover it all and to feed the vast and growing appetite of the Western public for news from Moscow. And then we get home to our friends and families and colleagues and they all ask us one question: 'What's it *really* like?'

And when the questioners go into detail, they usually ask what the night life is like? or can the Russians own property? or how cold and miserable are the winters? or what is a Russian wedding like? and does the state regiment everybody?

Answers to these and other fascinating questions, in response to widespread consumer demand, will be found in the following pages.

White knight to the rescue
5 November 1985

In Garry Kasparov's home town of Baku, there is a long, curving esplanade beside the shore of the Caspian dotted with small pavilions. They are laid out with neat rows of tables topped in black and white squares for chess-playing. But last weekend there was only one chess game in progress for every twenty games of backgammon.

The crowds outside the Tchaikovsky Hall where the world chess championship has been played, the media fuss, and the highly publicised animosity between Karpov and Kasparov, has served to give chess a prominence which it no longer really holds in Soviet society. It remains a vastly popular game, with some four million registered club players, and it has produced more than half of the world's stock of grandmasters, masters and international masters. But chess in the Soviet Union is now one sport among many, still dominant, but no longer the standard-bearer of Soviet culture that it was even twenty years ago.

Chess was deliberately cultivated after the Revolution as a means of bringing intellectual discipline to the workers, and showing the world what Soviet organization could do. The number of officially registered chess players rose from 1000 in 1924 to 500,000 by 1934.

The importance of chess was underlined by the relative weakness of the pre-war Soviet Union in other international sporting events. The post-war strength of Soviet sports in Olympic events has inevitably eroded the unique role that chess once enjoyed here. Moreover, the Russians stopped winning. The defeat of Boris Spassky by the American Bobby Fischer in 1972 was one blow, and the defeat of the Soviet international team by the Hungarians in 1978 was another.

The Soviet chess school owed its early success to its pioneer work in organizing the game. The regular competitions, the schools for young players and the whole-hearted support of the Soviet media created a unique forcing house for mass talent. And the Soviets also organized the theoretical development of chess.

These techniques have now been copied in other countries and much of the recent success of British chess depends on the skilful emulation of Soviet techniques, albeit with fewer resources and far less public support.

The popularity of chess has not faded in Russia so much as stopped growing at its earlier pace. Other sports and leisure pastimes have grown up to challenge it. But if anything can restore chess to its old primacy here, it is the mercurial character and dashing play of Garry Kasparov, who has caught the national imagination in a quite remarkable way.

Darkly handsome, enjoying a highly-visible affair with the beautiful actress Marina Neyolova, Kasparov's play is even more flamboyant than his private life. He has a killer instinct, a love of the bold sacrifice to build up his attack and a rare creative way with new twists to old openings.

Karpov, by comparison, is a bore. His support for official Soviet causes and the discretion of his personal life are like the cool, rather finicky chess that he plays. Karpov is too good to be true, and his chess mastery has been built on wresting wins from the tiniest of positional advantages, working and working away at the potential weakness until it becomes an open sore.

This image of the bloodless technocrat who says and does all the right things for the party is not popular in the Soviet Union, but his success as world champion, and his defeat of the defector Viktor Korchnoi has allowed Karpov to rebuild the structure of Soviet chess pretty much to his liking. His personal friends and attendants now dominate the organizing structure of the game, and give Karpov a weight in the international chess business which clearly worked to his advantage last February, when rules were bent to save him from what looked like inevitable defeat, and probably nervous breakdown.

But as well as these differences of personality, something political has entered into the battle between the two men. Karpov became world champion in the days of Brezhnev, and was taken up by the old leader as the very model of modern Soviet youth. Interestingly, the photograph of Karpov being embraced by Brezhnev has recently been removed from its pride of place at the Soviet chess HQ.

The political big guns now seem to be on Kasparov's side. Geidar Aliev, the Politburo member who used to run Kasparov's home state of Azerbaijan is a personal friend. When Kasparov was summoned to Moscow for a disciplinary hearing after speaking openly to Western journalists after last February's abortive championship, Aliev flew to Moscow with him, accompanied him to the hearing, and effectively ensured fair play from the disciplinary board, composed of Karpov's loyalists.

During the current championship, the new Foreign Minister, Eduard Shevardnadze, who comes from the Georgian republic next door to Azerbaijan, is said to have made a point of visiting the players backstage, shaking Kasparov warmly by the hand and ignoring Karpov.

Most Russians seem now to be rooting for Kasparov, who for so long was the underdog, and whose daring play, unconventional lifestyle and refusal to be brow-beaten by the old Soviet chess establishment typifies the changes that have started to come in Soviet life since Mr Gorbachev's new generation came to power.

Samovar cheer and a dacha white heaven

26 January 1985

It was 10°C below freezing, but after ten miles skiing along the flat trails of the forest, we were sweating freely when suddenly, through a break in the massed white columns of the birch trees, we saw the River Volga. As wide and flat and white as a wintry airfield, its expanse was dotted by small humped figures, the ice fishermen.

We ski'd, or rather ploughed, laboriously through the thick fresh snow to the nearest one, exchanged greetings and admired his catch: four small white fish with red fins and a red dusting on their backs. Beside them lay the enormous drill that the fishermen use to make a hole through the two feet of ice that covered the river.

He was wearing valenki, the thick felt boots that keep the feet warm through a long day on the ice, the kind favoured by Moscow traffic cops. He wore a fur hat and mittens, and an array of coats so thick that when he stood, his shape was a perfect sphere.

Sasha, the Russian friend who insisted that I learn to ski cross country, brushed the ice from his moustache and pointed far across the river. Look, he said, the dacha.

And there, humped under three feet of snow, the frost

curling thickly on the windows, stood the little wooden oasis of warmth with its double doors and double windows. And across from it stood the banya, the Russian bath house, with the tangled scars in the snow outside where we had rushed from the heat the previous evening and rolled exhilaratingly in the pure snow.

You have to be a Russian to pronounce the word 'dacha' properly. With all its overtones of home, of tradition, or spartan comfort and the almost mystic sense of communion that a Russian feels for his countryside. In English, it means simply a cottage, but to a Russian, a dacha is spring weekends that are thick with wild flowers, endless summer days and hunting for mushrooms, and above all, it means the delights of winter.

If there is any single thing that sets the Russians apart from Western Europeans, it is their attitude to winter. We tend to fear it, to shrink before the prospect of that much snow, that much numbing cold.

But the Russians embrace winter, look forward hungrily to the kind of sharp, brisk cold, clear skies and thick snow that we are enjoying now. The open spaces around Moscow are thick with skiers, skaters and grandparents doing their duty of introducing the young to winter's delights by hauling infants on sledges.

There are few places as lovely as a Russian forest in winter. The light can be at once soft and blindingly intense, from the snow at your feet to the whiteness of the birch trunks, and then the snow again lying thickly on the branches, sometimes dusted pink by the low winter sun.

The forests are a delight, the skiing a rare pleasure, but best of all is to ski back to a dacha, where the samovar will be bubbling with tea, the furnace in the banya is stoking furiously, and the ice cold vodka waiting.

Outside every Russian town, you see the dachas, rank upon rank of them like a British housing estate, except far more varied. They range from tiny wooden garden sheds, barely warmed by a wood-fuelled stove, to two-storeyed houses.

The varied design of the dachas is a striking example of individualism and diversity in the collective state, and most Russian families either have one, or are scheming and saving to get one. Dachas can be owned, as private property, and can be passed on to your heirs.

The grandest dachas of all are reserved for the élite. Some twenty miles outside Moscow is the village of Zhukovka, where the political and academic establishment have their state dachas, which go with their jobs and cannot be bequeathed to the children.

Writers tend to live around the village of Peredelkino. Foreign diplomats can rent dachas at Zavidovo, two hours' drive north from Moscow, where Leonid Brezhnev had a hunting lodge from which he indulged his passion for that other great sport of the Russians.

Sometimes while skiing, you see the hunters moving silently through the woods in their white hoods and smocks, their guns slung over their shoulders, just like the wartime photos of the defence of Moscow. And one of Moscow's most popular shops is Alyen ('Game') on Leninsky Prospekt, where you can buy venison and wild duck, partridges and hares for a classic winter's feast.

After we had ski'd across the Volga, and after our bath and the inevitable roll in the snow, Sasha took me to a friend's dacha for dinner. Simon is a hunter, and he served us venison he had shot himself, cooked with onions and a little garlic. We drank vodka and Simon told us of hunting moose, or of his autumn trips to Siberia to hunt bear and wildcats.

When we left, it was 15° below, the trees glowed a fierce white in their frost and the clear sky was ablaze with stars. 'Winter,' said Sasha, sniffing the cold air exultantly. 'The finest time of year. The skiing will be good tomorrow.'

The red brick lesson

20 October 1986

My friend Yuri owns his own apartment. A standard three-room Moscow flat, it is worth about 20,000 roubles these days. Only one in six Muscovites are so lucky.

When he bought it, about ten years ago, it was valued at 12,000 roubles, and he had to put down the minimum deposit of one third of the value. He then borrowed the rest of the money from the state as a mortgage, which he repays over twenty years at an interest rate of 2 per cent.

His monthly payments are about 45 roubles, compared to the 10–12 roubles he would pay in rent for a council flat. And in ten years' time, he will have a significant asset.

When he dies, his children can inherit the flat. If they do not want it, they can sell it. The only catch to all this is that the whole block of flats is a co-operative, and the rest of the co-op must approve any prospective purchaser who wants to buy in.

Like most foreigners, I was startled when I learned about the prevalence of home ownership in the Soviet state. But it makes a great deal of sense for the system. First, the payment of the deposits eases the state's own housing budget, and second, people buying their own co-ops are customers taken out of the long queue for public housing.

This co-op system of housing has had a chequered history. It began with Lenin's new economic policy after the civil war in 1921, when he licensed small-scale capitalism and commerce in an effort to rebuild a war-shattered economy. Stalin stopped it in the 1930s, and it was revived under Krushchev as a component of his crash housing programme.

It has never worked quite as well as intended, and these days just over 10 per cent of new flats are built as co-ops. Every year *Pravda* runs a mournful piece saying the plan for co-ops has not been met again.

The reason for this is not a shortage of cash. There are 1.3 million families on the waiting list to buy a co-op flat, but less than 150,000 of them are built each year – which makes the co-op waiting list almost as long as the list for public housing.

The main reason for the delay is that the construction teams do not like to build for co-ops, who are more finicky customers, want better quality, and are much less ready than the state to sign the formal papers saying that the place has been received in good order.

This means that the builders risk losing their bonuses for completion on time. To solve this, a new regulation has been brought into force this year in twenty big cities, which says that instead of ordering their apartment block from scratch co-ops can buy completed blocks in newly-built housing complexes.

In effect, it means the builders will not know whether their clients are public or private, and it will probably also mean that the co-op owners will have to take care of the finishing themselves.

The other problem is that these co-ops are hardly ever individual families who decide to club together to fund an apartment block. They need an official sponsor, and this is almost always their place of work, whether a ministry, a factory, a trading enterprise, or an academic institute.

Opposite my own home on Serpukhovsky Val is a co-op for local families, and my friend Yuri lives in a co-op sponsored by his research institute. In the quarter near the *Pravda* press complex, there are co-ops for journalists and print workers, and the union of artists has several co-ops.

These sponsoring organizations are supposed to fund the connection of 'their' apartment blocks to city services like the sewers and water supplies, to pay for access roads, and the like. Since they are reluctant to pay the full price, and the city housing department will not pick up the tab, most co-ops either remain half-finished or force the members to club together to make up the difference.

But over the years, as co-op members die and their heirs sell, the once-coherent population of each of the blocks starts to change. They have less and less in common, no longer all work at the same place, and steadily become strangers to each other. Partly because of this, there is now talk of reviving the old 1920s co-op residential unions to give them more muscle when arguing with the city council over major repairs, bus routes, local shops, and services.

It is one of the many surprising ironies of the Soviet system that the only other places I know where this kind of co-op housing flourishes are in the capitalist bastions of New York and London, where, of course, they are known as condominiums and housing associations.

Poet in the house

1 December 1986

One of the cleverest young Russians I know is a Dvornik, a kind of caretaker of a block of flats. His name is Stas, and he is more conscientious than most. He actually sweeps away the snow from the yard of his block, mends fuses and does some handyman repairs. But mainly he just writes his poetry.

He speaks four languages, paints well, and has a good degree from Moscow University. He can tan the hide off me at chess, and if he wanted to use the family connections to help his career, he has an uncle who is a general.

But Stas does not care. He just wants time to do his own work, and is prepared to live what is by Soviet standards a pretty menial life in order to be left alone. He has a job, so he cannot be accused of parasitism. He has a small legal salary, way down below the poverty level of 100 roubles a month.

The more I think about this, I know an alarming number of people like Stas. There is an underground rock musician I know whose formal job is to be a nurse in a kindergarten. He wants no more than that, and the freedom to get on with his music.

There are a couple of people I know, avant-garde composers who live on the 70 roubles a month they get as the lowest grade of music teacher. And at parties, in cafes, I meet people of obvious brains and energy who hold undemanding or purely nominal jobs, as bus cleaners, night watchmen and kiosk attendants.

There are others who work for a year or two in Siberia to earn the big bonuses and then spend months on the Black Sea coast on the proceeds. But Stas and those like him are something else – drop outs who have reached a stable and accommodating but arm's length relationship with the Soviet system.

I used to think that knowing so many of these types was something to do with my being a foreigner, or with my own tastes for the cultural fringe. In any event, I thought it was a social phenomenon of the big cities, and the young intelligentsia.

Not so, as I found from that impeccable source *Kommunist*, the official ideological journal of the party's Central Committee. Ever since the 27th Party Congress, when the old editor Richard Kosolapov was replaced by Ivan Frolov, this 'theoretical and political organ' has started to read a bit like a samizdat (underground newspaper).

One of the most interesting and boldest of the Siberian school of economists, Tataiana Zaslavskaya, has published in *Kommunist* a long essay on the human factor in economic reform, and identified this problem of the lack of ambition as increasingly characteristic of Soviet society in general.

She referred to a survey carried out among senior and middle rank managers on Siberian collective farms. Only 9 per cent of the top managers and only 13 per cent of middle managers wanted to carry on up the ladder of responsibility. Indeed, 30 per cent of the senior managers, and a staggering 70 per cent of middle managers wanted 'lower-ranking posts'.

'This was not because they were unable to cope with their work,' Ms Zaslavskaya went on. 'This migration of qualified engineers and technicians into workers' positions confirms the incapacity of our existing managerial systems to deploy effectively the human resources of our society . . . It is a paradox of our time.'

One reason for this is that because of the new patterns of work on the farms, with more encouragement for private plots and 'brigade teams' of virtually self-employed farm workers whose pay is linked directly to productivity, the farm labourers can now earn very much more than the farm managers.

But Zaslavskaya goes on to argue that this voluntary de-skilling or reluctance to face the responsibilities that should go with one's qualifications, was widespread in industry too. She even referred to the 'striving of the managerial cadres not to rise up the ladder, not to expand the focus of their initiative, but rather narrow it.'

What all this means is that an alarmingly large and economically crucial fraction of Soviet society has gone on a kind of soft strike. They are not, in Lenin's words voting with their feet, but rather voting with the very reluctance of their ambition. No wonder Gorbachev is spending so much time on television and stomping the country to exhort the masses. If he cannot energize and inspire them, and woo them with cultural thaws, this soft strike of the intelligentsia and managers will frustrate all his plans.

A nasty sight in a Soviet
25 May 1987

Some ten years ago, I published a book on Britain's neo-fascists, the National Front, and one place I never expected to encounter the breed again was Moscow. But here they are in Russian form, with their anti-semitism, their conspiracy theories and their frightening, mystic chauvinism.

They go by the name of 'Pamyat', which means memory,. or heritage. On the face of it, Pamyat appears to be a grassroots movement of conservationists with the admirable goal of preserving Russia's historic monuments.

Two weeks ago, they organized a public demonstration in the heart of Moscow, marched on City Hall and demanded a meeting with Boris Yeltsin, the party chief of the capital, and one of Gorbachev's most passionate supporters. He met them, answered their questions, and by all accounts was appalled at what he heard of their views.

Now the Soviet press has started to probe Pamyat and found some nasty things. *Komsomolskaya Pravda* sent along a reporter to its meetings. After reading her account and then on going quietly along to one of their sessions, I felt myself carried back in time to those NF rallies in Britain ten years ago.

Who was to blame for the destruction of old Russian monuments, was the theme of one meeting. Kaganovich, whose father's name was Moses, and Yaroslavsky, whose real name was Gubelman, came the reply. 'And we all know what those names mean,' sneered the speaker.

'It is the non-Russians, those not in our Orthodox church, the freemasons, who destroy our Orthodox monuments,' claimed one of the Pamyat leaders, Vasiliev by name. 'A whole caste has grown up of people who insult us and live off the people's money. They do not understand anything, all they can do is defile our national heritage.'

'All of you good Russians in the audience, every third one of you has the brains of a genius. That's a scientific fact. But they have not allowed you to reveal your genius, these Imperialist and Zionist agents who conspire through bureaucracy. These people who are ruining our economy and our society are being allowed to retire on pension. They ought to be shot.'

At another meeting, held in a Komsomol hall, that same Vasiliev announced the start of a campaign to get another Pamyat leader, Konstantin Andreyev, nominated as a candidate for the regional Soviet.

It was time, he argued, for Pamyat to put its views and candidates before the electors, almost as an act of self-defence. 'The propaganda department of our Moscow city party committee is sticking political labels on to us. If they do not stop, we shall use the criminal code and charge them with slander. But the floods of cosmopolitanism have swept through so much of our national life, into our mass media. Take rock music – that is Satanism, they swear oaths of loyalty to Satan,' Vasiliev went on.

The meeting went on to discuss the building of the hugely unpopular Victory monument on the Poklonnaya hills outside Moscow (which the government has now stopped).

'If you go along there, you will see how many of the buildings contain Masonic and Zionist symbols. They are everywhere. This is how the werewolves of art operate,' we were told. One of the Pamyat council members, introduced as V. Vinogradov, then spoke at length on the theme of Moscow as 'the third Rome, the heavenly city, the world's most holy place.'

After Rome, the centre of the empire and orthodoxy had shifted to Byzantium, but the rape of the centre of the Eastern church by the Islamic invaders had meant that the heart of Christian civilization had shifted to Moscow, the third Rome, the new seat of empire.

This was heady stuff, the kind of mystic bombast I had last come across in reading the works of the nineteenth century Slavophiles, who denounced Peter the Great and his attempts to open Holy Mother Russia to the dangerous, free-thinking and free-trading West.

Komsomolskaya Pravda attacked them for 'a shameless (or illiterate) linking of Leninism to the Pamyat leaders' platform: a shameless mixture of clericalism and mysticism with "Leninism" is characteristic of their speeches.'

Indeed it is, but the real significance of the emergence of Pamyat is that the Gorbachev reforms and glasnost are coming up against that age-old problem, that freedom of speech means freedom for the extremist, as well as the liberal. Lifting the stones from Soviet society is allowing some unpleasant things to crawl out.

Ones that get away
8 June 1987

Now that we have all digested the one year anniversary of Chernobyl, there is one curious feature of the entire affair that has almost been forgotten. I think of it as the case of the disappearing technicians, and it offers an interesting insight into the nature of what the West tends to see as the world's ultimate police state.

On June 15 last year, *Pravda* ran a long account of the way that almost the entire management team of the Chernobyl power station had been fired for 'irresponsibility and lack of control'. And it went on to say that several Chernobyl technicians, including shift supervisors, foremen and senior operators, 'are to be found on the run'.

In fact, they disappeared, and there has been no indication to this day that they have ever been found. This raises all sorts of intriguing questions. In the chaos of the month after Chernobyl, with hundreds of thousands of people being evacuated and resettled, one can comprehend people being able to disappear. But how long can they keep it up, in a country with restrictions on internal travel, an ubiquitous police system, and where all sorts of official documents are requested to get a job, a flat or even a hotel room?

I used to wonder how Moscow's hippies could get by, without the residential papers that give them the right to stay in the capital. Or how so many of the people around the rock scene could live without any visible means of support, moving on from one friend's flat to another and pottering around the country without any identity documents at all.

The answer is easy enough. The Soviet Union is a vast place, and between the corruption and the inefficiency and the limits on police powers, there are endless ways of slipping through the net of official control.

Siberia is still the wild west, so short of labour that in many factories people can get jobs with no questions being asked. Throughout the forest fire season of the summer, there is work as a temporary fireman. There is a permanent shortage of stevedores in the Siberian river ports.

And all over the country, the mobile groups of self-employed workers called 'shabashniki' usually have a place for a skilled hand. For a fixed sum payable in cash, they build the roads and the barns and the new storehouses and accommodation that the collective farms require, and which would take months or years to have constructed through the state system.

The traditional internal passport system has loosened to the point where anyone can spend a few days visiting friends or family, even in tightly-controlled Moscow, without needing to get any official permission. Although you have to show some kind of identifying document to buy an air ticket, cash alone will do for train tickets, or for journeys by riverboat.

The police controls of movement around this vast country are nothing like as strict in practice as they are in theory. I sometimes go off on the organized hikes around Moscow laid on by self-appointed guides. We meet up at a particular station platform at a given hour early on a Saturday morning, take the train to the country and spend the day walking the 1941 battlefields, or just hiking.

And usually, when I check the map, I find that our route has paid little attention to that strict rule that says we foreigners have to notify the authorities two days in advance if we want to venture more than 40 kilometres from the Kremlin. I have never yet seen a police check, nor had my papers or identity questioned. And I recently came across another illuminating example of the holes in the system of state control in the pages of *Sozialisticheskaya Industria*. One of its bold reporters had joined the police on one of their regular monthly raids on the vast 100-acre garbage dump at Electric Corner, just north of Moscow, where hundreds of vagabonds live all year round.

On the raid he described, they picked up forty-two men and women, lacking papers, and some of them were arrested for the fifth and sixth times. Some of them lived in cardboard shanties, some in caves in the ground, and others had carefully camouflaged huts deep in the nearby forest.

In Russian slang, they are known as the 'bomzhi', from the legal phrase that means of no fixed abode. And although everyone has known of them for years, and owners of burgled dachas tend to blame them for the new spurt in rural crime, this is the first time the existence of these Soviet tramps has been acknowledged in print. Another victory for glasnost. And who knows? If they keep looking, one day they might catch up with the disappeared technicians of Chernobyl.

Moulin red

7 September 1987

They call it the best night club west of Tokyo, and for about 5000 miles there is not a great deal of competition. Way out in Moscow's northern suburbs, far from the tourist zones, stands the plush new Soyuz (Union) Hotel, with its huge restaurant, and daring, dazzling floor show that would not look out of place at the Crazy Horse in Paris.

But the Soyuz is the Russians' own night spot. It is not an Intourist hotel, geared to milking Western tourists of their precious hard currency. Westerners who live in Moscow get to hear of the place only from Russian friends who are in the know, because the Soyuz is where the demi-monde of the Moscow élite goes for its kicks.

The audience included former Bolshoi dancers who have 'married well', as they say here, the sons and daughters of top Kremlin officials, and Moscow's new rich. In one corner, there was the composer of glutinous popular ballads, and in another, a sleek Armenian restaurant boss, his solid gold Cartier watch gleaming beneath the silk cuff, and his wife decked out in diamonds so big you could see her wrists strain. When complimented on her dress, she said airily: 'It's from Paris, they do them so well there.'

The tables groaned under the most lavish array of caviare, smoked salmon and sturgeon, roast beef and confections of ham in aspic. The new campaign against alcohol was evidently having little effect, the bottles of Soviet champagne, vodka and Armenian cognac were emptying fast.

At 8.30 precisely, the floor show began, a rather good rock band playing soft chords around a giant golden samovar, and the first dancers paraded slowly into the room. They were long, leggy blondes, dressed in traditional Russian head-dresses and colourful robes that stretched down, barely, to their rumps.

They were followed by the Armenian dancers, black-eyed beauties in the kind of diaphanous, flowing skirts and skimpy bras that bring back memories of steamy belly dancers. Their partners wore the tightest of black tights, danced bare-chested and won sighs of approval from the women in the audience. The dance was superbly done, suggestive and graceful at the same time.

Then came the medieval tumblers complete with dancing bear, romantic love songs, rumbustious choruses, a magic cat, and a magnificent blonde with hair down to her knees in a skin-tight golden cat suit that served to emphasize her endowments. There were chorus dancers dressed in vast butterfly wings that loomed over low cut costumes of pearls and paste jewels and there were exotic head-dresses. Interweaved with all this was a thin, but ideologically correct plot, about a buffoon of a king who was trying to steal the innocent bride of a fine Russian boy, until the magic cat and Moscow's busty version of Tina Turner found a way to make all end happily. With a considerable stretch of the imagination, you could have seen the cat as an allegory for the Communist Party, saving young marital innocence from a lecherous monarchy. Or at least, you could until the finale when the cat leaped out from the giant golden samovar.

'You should have seen it eighteen months ago,' one of my friends said when the applause died down. 'Before all this new puritanism came in. The costumes could have come from Paris. There were G-strings, the dancers were more lascivious. We used to get off-duty policemen in the audience.'

The customers began to dance to a melody of jazzed-up Soviet tunes, and remarkably good versions of Michael Jackson, U-2 and Bruce Springsteen. Like any louche night club anywhere on earth, the dance floor was filled with middle-aged men dancing with pretty girls, and stunningly-dressed plain women dancing with handsome young men.

A Moscow millionaire told me about the Soyuz. He made his money from Magnetizdat, which is like samizdat publishing with cassette tapes instead of manuscripts. He obtained new Western records, and had a small studio with banks of cassette machines that turned out hundreds of copies of the latest Western music, and a small printing machine to produce uncannily genuine-looking labels.

I looked out for him among the tables. But he was not in the cheery wedding group, nor at the table with the Libyan diplomats with the pretty Russian girls, not even at the handful of tables where stolid Russian foursomes were having the time of their lives, paying about £20 a head for the best restaurant fare and night club entertainment that Moscow has to offer. What they had to pay, or what strings they had to pull to get a table, would be something else again.

Blues for the bride

19 October 1987

Being already and happily married, I never expected to experience a Soviet wedding from the inside. But a very close friend asked me to be his 'shaffer', or best man. And so last Friday, bearing armfuls of flowers and with our daughters acting as bridesmaids, we turned up at 2.45 p.m. outside the Department of Registration for Civic and State Acts of the Executive Committee of the Sevastopol District of the Soviet of Peoples' Deputies of Moscow, at 9 Trade Union Street.

It was locked. So while others went off to investigate, I and the matron of honour were draped with red sashes. The back door was found to be open, so we went past the little stall selling grapes, past the dustbins and into the wedding palace. On our left was the bride's room. It contained a long mirror, a single chair, four fluorescent lamps, and that was all. There was no table or coat hook, not even a window. Straight ahead were the lavatories, and on our right, a small hall outside the Office of Registration where the ceremony was to take place.

Two families were already waiting, and another wedding was already under way inside. It was very quiet. Just by the door was a notice, charmingly illustrated with bunches of flowers. It read: 'Honoured young ones. We ask you to hand over your passports to the Department of Documentation. In the mirrored room, you may order photographs and musical accompaniment to your wedding. The event will last 30–40 minutes.' We did not find the mirrored room, and there was no musical accompaniment.

When our turn came in the tiny office, we were told: 'It is forbidden to photograph during the signing of documents.' This was said by the middle-aged lady who was to perform the marriage act. She had a pen with a panda's head on top, and several imposing stamps on the table, and piles of documents.

Art and Svetlana, the happy couple, handed over their passports, and the lady checked their details against the marriage application forms. She then put a large stamp in each passport and filled in the details of the new spouse. She then filled out the marital registration form, which I and the matron of honour had to sign as adult witnesses of good character that our friends Art and Svetlana were indeed who they purported to be, that they were of sound mind, and that the wedding had been performed in our presence. The lady then stood up, and formally asked the happy couple if they sincerely wanted to enter the state of matrimony. They each said yes, and then she filled out a small but rather impressive-looking embossed booklet. These were the marriage lines.'I formally congratulate you on your marriage, and in the name of the people of the hero-city of Moscow, wish you long health, happiness, children and success,' she said, and this time we could take photographs and kiss each other, and my children handed over more bouquets to the bride.

All this had taken perhaps fifteen minutes, inside a room that measured four metres square, which was mainly filled by the desk and three chairs. I think it was a special favour to a foreigner that persuaded the lady to let our children and Art's father into the ceremony. We then left the room, put our coats on, and walked out of the back door, while the children surprised everybody by tossing handfuls of rice at the bride and groom.

It is possible to have a rather grander wedding, with the bride in a long white dress, and chaika limousines hired for the day to take the new bride on to toss her bouquet onto the Tomb of the Unknown Soldier at the corner of the Kremlin. In the days when it was legal to drink alcohol in the open air, people would often go up to the Lenin Hills by the university and drink a champagne toast while gazing out over the vast spread of Moscow. But these days, the visit to the Lenin Hills is simply one page of the wedding photo album.

The real ceremony took place that evening, at the wedding party at the flat where Art and Svetlana live. He is a musician and journalist, whose book on the history of Soviet rock *Back in the USSR* is about to be published in Britain by Omnibus Press. She is a designer and fashion writer, and one of the loveliest women in Moscow. Their party saw the gathering of Soviet youth culture. Boris Grebenshikov, the lead singer from Aquarium, whose lyrics make him one of the outstanding young poets of the day, had flown down from Leningrad. Andrei Reutter, the young Moscow artist whose canvases sell for thousands of dollars in the US, was chatting with Pavel, literary critic and the youngest full professor at Moscow University. It was a wonderful party that went on till dawn, but as five-year-old Kate had asked me after throwing the rice, 'Daddy, when will the real wedding be?'

6
Media

The first Russian word of the Gorbachev era to enter Western vocabularies was 'glasnost'. This was because the transformation of the Soviet press was the first unmistakable sign that Gorbachev meant business when he promised to overhaul the entire Soviet system. It was also the easiest place to start. Economic reform takes a long time, but newspapers can be transformed almost overnight.

But if they had been transformed overnight, it would have been deeply suspicious, as if the great press baron in the Kremlin had uttered the word 'glasnost' and like a vast army, the whole Soviet media had wheeled and marched as one in the new direction. Then glasnost would have been nothing but a more palatable and more sophisticated way of spreading the news the Kremlin wanted the people to know.

But it did not work like that. Not quite. Papers like *Moscow News* and magazines like *Ogonyok* took risks and pushed the boundaries of glasnost forward, while *Pravda* lumbered along far behind, and other papers like the trade union daily *Trud* did not appear to have noticed that anything much had changed. And regional and local papers remained timid – were far more restrained – as Gorbachev occasionally complained.

On TV and radio, there were ghettos of glasnost. Youth programmes and late-night talk shows and some investigative TV journalism on the Moscow city channel were remarkable, and half the city would get home early from parties to watch. But most of Soviet TV remained the same boring and traditional diet of Soviet war movies, film of combine harvesters at work, folk dances and televised speeches.

It was not easy to tell what the viewers thought, because there is no such thing as a ratings system in the Soviet Union, because there are no advertisers clamouring to know how big an audience they get for their money. But the sharp rise in circulation of the main papers and magazines in the first two years of glasnost was the best possible proof that the Soviet public liked it, was fascinated by the process, and wanted more.

Mating calls
9 June 1986

If any British lonely hearts are interested in a divorced tractor driver with his own motorbike in the picturesque Altai foothills in southern Siberia, we may be able to help.

And there is a female non-smoking supervisor of a sanatorium on the Baltic coast who is looking for a teetotal gentleman of mature years who is fond of classical music. Must be fluent in Russian and Latvian, and preferably have his own car.

But this month's star attraction is a first mate on a Murmansk-based fish factory-ship, due to retire in four years, who is looking for an attractive lady in her thirties who would like to share his well-gotten gains. He does not put it like that, but he does mention his co-op flat in Leningrad, his own car, and his own dacha on the Baltic. The fishermen earn good money, and spend long enough at sea to save it.

The lonely hearts ads in the Soviet press are not easy to find. But the local newspapers in two far-flung cities print special supplements for them, and as a result, these otherwise obscure publications – from Alma-Ata near the Chinese border and Riga on the Baltic coast – are devoured across the entire Soviet Union.

In Moscow, you can expect to pay a healthy premium on the cover price just to look at a copy overnight. Indeed, even the much more boring classified ad supplement of the Moscow papers takes some finding. The local evening paper, *Vechernaya Moskva*, prints the supplement 78 times a year, with a print run of 350,000 copies, and although it does not contain lonely hearts, it is sold out as soon as it goes on sale.

The eight-page supplement is dominated by the housing market. There are dachas for sale or rent, people wanting to sub-let flats, or to exchange them. The ad supplement is so much part of the city's folklore that it even figures in the latest joke, about the ad that offers to exchange a three-room flat in Chernobyl for anything anywhere – except in Hiroshima or Nagasaki.

But slowly, as the habit of advertising catches on, the ads are becoming a fascinating chronicle of the patterns of social change. This week, there are two offering to buy personal computers – even if not in working order. Video and tape-recorders are also solicited, working or broken. There is a motor-boat with its own mooring place on offer, a home-gymnasium, a Becker grand piano and a big fridge-freezer.

The freezer was 18,000 roubles, or nine months' average pay, and it had been sold by the time I rang, about four hours after the paper hit the streets. The number selling the video recorder was permanently engaged.

My favourite item was the mammoth tusk, on a chrome metal stand. 'It's a lovely piece,' said the voice on the phone, 'Got its own chrome metal stand, 1 metre 38 long, 40 centimetres diameter, in lovely condition.

'It came from Marina Rosha about thirty years ago, from a real archaeology expedition, but that was bandit country in those days, and it's been in the family ever since. It's a real snip at 1500 roubles,' he said, in the kind of voice that in England would call you 'Squire'.

I said that was a bit more than I could manage. 'Well what about something cheaper. I can do you a whale's jaw at 3 roubles, or a lovely set of antlers at 150 roubles. If you want something smaller, I've got a walrus tooth. What about some real ostrich feathers ...'

But the real sign of social change is the great rash of ads for a nanny to look after the children of the increasingly affluent middle classes. This is now such a sellers' market that the ads cringe and wheedle. 'Visits to family dacha guaranteed,' is a common incentive. There are ads for housekeepers – the word maid or servant is taboo – and a carefully worded plea for a 'house-worker' to help someone complete a self-built dacha.

If you want a summer job, there are vacancies for ice-cream sellers in the Crimea, and factories and enterprises are taking advantage of their new post-Gorbachev economic freedoms to sell off surplus goods. The Rossia Hotel is offering unwanted furniture, and the State Alcohol Board is offering 200,000 empty brandy bottles.

All these are things to gladden Mr Gorbachev's reforming heart, but given his concern about the shortcomings of the Soviet service sector, he will be delighted by the ad from the Chaika Dry-Cleaning Co-operative, which announces the launch of a new home delivery and pick up service. A Moscow lonely hearts column cannot be far away.

Olga's beef
11 August 1985

A friend of mine is an indefatigable writer of letters to the Soviet press, largely because she is convinced they work. Her first effort came after a visit to the Moscow zoo, and she was heartbroken by the cramped cages and generally downcast air of the animals, located near one of the busiest traffic junctions in the city.

She wrote to *Vechernaya Moskva* and within ten days had received a formal letter from the Ministry of Culture, asking her to visit the zoo again. She was met by the deputy director, a vet and a young official of the ministry, and taken on a guided tour while the vet explained how the animals' health was monitored, and the deputy director spoke of his own concern, and his faith in the rebuilding project which would house all the animals better in the future.

My friend Olga thought this was rather impressive. She worked, by the way, as a secretary and can claim no status or influence. She had written the letter from home as an ordinary citizen.

She later spent about a month's salary on an imported

Finnish raincoat, bought quite openly at a Moscow department store, and was delighted with its chic cut and style. Then she sent it to be cleaned. Disaster. It needed a special dry-cleaning process, and the Moscow dry cleaners had none of the required chemicals.

This time she wrote to *Rabochnitsa*, a magazine which translates as 'working woman'. It is ridiculous, she began, that our Ministry of Foreign Trade should pay the Finns for clothes we cannot clean. Either we should not buy them at all, or we should buy the chemicals to clean them at the same time.

This time she received a duplicated letter, which had obviously been sent out to hundreds of other complainants, from the Moscow trade department which had been responsible for selling the coats. It was apologetic in tone, and said that arrangements had been made with the Ministry of Foreign Trade to buy not only Finnish dry-cleaning chemicals, but also some Finnish dry-cleaning machines that would solve the problem of the disappointed purchasers.

This, Olga dismissed as a 'skoro budit' – brush-off. Skoro budit means 'it will happen soon', and is the Russian equivalent of *manyana*. She was right. A year later, she still cannot get her coat cleaned.

But her faith in the letters system is unshaken, and her next one was a humdinger.

'We can buy German-made coats of our good Russian fur in our shops for 12,000 roubles,' she began. 'It takes me over five years to earn that much money and I cannot afford it, but it is good that people who can afford it should be able to make such a purchase. But if our trading department is imaginative enough to provide such luxuries, why cannot they provide any of our shops with a decent Soviet-made deodorant selling for two roubles, which is what women really need.'

She sat back to await results, sure that the shelves of GUM would soon overflow with deodorant, and that she might even be escorted round by a pleasant young man from the Ministry of Light Industry.

Instead, she received a personal letter from the head of the letters department at *Rabochnitsa*. It read, in full: 'Thank you for your letter, which will help us in our efforts to wage our joint campaign against shortages.'

It seems the letters pages of the newspapers, the much vaunted safety-valve of the Soviet system, are being clogged with too many complaints. Party officials are already talking openly of the new wave of criticisms unleashed by Gorbachev having gone too far; that people are complaining about flippant things; that enterprising managers are spending far too much of their time dealing with press inquiries into letters complaining that the manager is arrogant and resists constructive criticism.

The letters department of *Moskovskaya Pravda*, for example, used to receive about 150 letters a day. This time last year, the figure was up to 300, and now it approaches 500 a day. They have to take on part-time worker-correspondents to help cope with the flood.

Reporters at other newspapers say it is happening there too, and the letters department of the Central Committee has also noted a sharper rise in its volume of mail from the public. *Pravda* wearily reported last week that not a day went past without its office in Alma-Ata getting written complaints about corruption, bad food supplies and the like.

At one level, this means more disappointments for Olga and her fellow letter-writers, and, perhaps, the disillusion of their faith that the system can be responsive. At another level, and more ominously, we are seeing the first signs of the official backlash against the Gorbachev reforms. Incidentally, not one of Olga's letters was ever printed.

Street of pride
25 August 1986

If I were the editor of *Izvestia*, I should be getting distinctly worried by now. The newspapers and the editors of the Soviet Union do not stand or fall by their circulation figures, but *Izvestia*'s decline in sales over recent years has become a distinct embarrassment.

Circulation is now down to a mere 6.4 million copies a day. This may sound a lot, but it represents a sad decline for a paper that in its good old days managed to sell over 10 million copies a day, and outsell *Pravda* too.

The good old days were the Krushchev period, when Krushchev's son-in-law Alexei Adzhubei was the editor. This did not mean the *Izvestia* began printing Kremlin leaks and won readers through its scoops. For Soviet newspapers, the key factor in circulation is the allocation of newsprint, which is decided by the authorities.

But newspapers being newspapers, and journalists being journalists, a little bit of healthy competition does creep into the business. And since *Pravda* is the official organ of the Central Committee (or the party) and *Izvestia* is published with the authority of the Supreme Soviet (or the government), one can occasionally detect some of that house loyalty which so enlivened relations between the Musketeers of the King of France and Cardinal Richelieu and of which one Alexandre Dumas made such a gripping yarn.

But if there is a d'Artagnan in the Soviet press corps, he is to be found neither at *Pravda* nor at *Izvestia*. Indeed, like most of the best journalists, he has been promoted out of the business in which he made his name.

Mikhail Nenashev was the editor of *Sovyetskaya Rossiya*, the paper that was founded thirty years ago by Adzhubei as the organ of the Russian Republic. Nenashev made it into the best, most readable and most forthright paper in the country, even though its status as a republican, rather than a national, paper has kept its circulation down to a humble 3.6 million.

After running an increasingly successful campaign against censorship, and to win his journalists the right to print critical stories before showing them to the party officials being criticized, Nenashev has now been promoted to be head of the state committee for publishing, printing and the book trade. And in spite of his paper's tiny circulation, this is a serious loss to Soviet journalism, which is a much more varied and even competitive trade than it appears on the surface.

You may not think it, to look at the depressingly similar pages, with their identical communiques from the Central Committee and identical texts of Mikhail Gorbachev's speeches, but there is a distinct difference between the pops and the qualities in the Soviet press.

The pale *Sun* of Soviet journalism is the paper published by the Trade Union Council, called *Trud* (labour). It has the highest circulation in the country, 18.6 million copies a day, and it has won them through sensationalism. Faith healing, UFOs, folk medicine, regular re-discoveries of Atlantis, and other dubious lost civilizations – these are the staples of the Soviet mass market.

The next big seller is *Komsomolskaya Pravda*, organ of the Young Communist League, with 13.6 million, probably because it prints rather more about rock music than the other papers. And on one famous occasion it began to double its print run when one of its enterprising reporters found, in the wilds of Siberia, a family of Old Believers who had fled religious persecution in the Tsar's time. They had never heard of Lenin, did not know that the revolution had taken place, knew nothing of railroads or electricity, and fled in alarm from the helicopter which found them. The paper's serial on them kept the entire country enthralled for weeks.

Pravda itself has the third highest circulation, with 10.4 million, and is just starting to recover from a long decline in sales. It will probably soon be overtaken by *Selskaya Zhizn* (village life), the fast-growing paper aimed at the farming community which yet has one of the best foreign pages, thanks largely to its enterprising foreign editor, Nikolai Pastukhov, a former *Pravda* correspondent in India.

The specialist papers have much smaller circulations. The military newspaper *Krasnaya Zvezda* (red star) sells just over two million copies a day, and *Sozialicheskaya Industria* manages just 1.2 million. Rather to my surprise, given the national passion for sports, *Sovyeski Sport* sells only 4.6 million a day.

Oddly, *Pravda*'s circulation does not rise much on Mondays, when it has the monopoly of being the only paper on sale. This is because most Russians buy their paper by subscription, and have it delivered, and make their choice of daily paper for the full year ahead.

Paper chase
22 December 1986

When I arrived in Moscow to open the *Guardian* bureau, just over two years ago, a veteran colleague warned me glumly that the great problem would be to find anything to write about.

'You'll spend your days reading through all the papers wondering what little news snippet you can find to make into something interesting,' he said. 'It's a way of passing the time between the deaths at the Kremlin.'

It has not quite been like that, because the biggest and most dramatic sign of change in my time in the Soviet Union has been the revolution which has taken place in the newspapers. The problem these days is choosing which of the endless stories that pour from the press I should investigate further. But every day, some corking stories just disappear into my files.

Take just one day this week. We begin with a story in *Izvestia*, the evening paper, about a programme on the local TV station in Georgia. It is a televised auction of consumer goods for which there is no demand. The trick is that the goods go to the viewer who calls in with the lowest bid.

This has been such a success in exposing shoddy and unwanted goods that the programme is now going to be screened on national TV.

Then I turned to *Trud*, the trade union paper which has the largest circulation in the country. This has been secured by the good old Fleet Street principle of sensation, in a staid Soviet style.

There was a story about a new glasnost telephone line open to the public in Vorkuta, a grim place in North Siberia which is notorious as the site of some of Stalin's worst labour camps. Glasnost began as the word to define Mr Gorbachev's encouragement of outspokenness in the media, but has now become a national catch-phrase for the right to sound off about almost anything.

In Vorkuta, you can now dial 70.707 and 'express your views on any problem that is bothering you, ask for a situation to be explained'. Your call will be taken by 'a qualified representative of the socio-psychological service'.

On the next page of *Trud* was a story about the bribery network being run by the traffic police in Saratov on the Volga river. There was a nice account of a taxi-driver who was stopped by the traffic police, told he had committed an offence, and they were about to punch a hole in his driving licence. Three holes mean suspension.

Instead, the police suggested, he might care to go to a nearby restaurant and bring back some shashlik. He did, but brought two witnesses as well, and then brought charges against the cops. At least this had stopped what the locals called the evening taxi parade, *Trud* commented, when at the end of the police shift, a long line of cabs would wait outside the police station to give the cops free rides home.

On another page was a tasty tale of enforced kick-backs in the Bolshoi orchestra. One of the violinists complained at having to donate part of his foreign currency allowance to an official – and found his job being advertised when they got back to Moscow. He had lost his musical skills, went the official explanation.

Then *Sozialicheskaya Industria* carried a good story about the corrupt police who ran a black market operation at a ball-bearing plant in Michurinsk. The police got local criminals to bully workers into stealing bearings, and when the goods were handed over, the cops would appear and demand a bribe.

In *Sovietskaya Kultura*, the film director Pavel Chukhrai had an angry piece about the way the country was losing its sense of respect for the dead. 'At the Donskoi monastery, the graves of the heroes of the 1812 war against Napoleon are in danger – there are plans to dig them up. And now that they close down the Novodevichy monastery, except to those with a special pass, this no longer seems immoral to us. We have got used to such things … and so when I think of Chernobyl, of the *Admiral Nakhimov* shipping disaster, I have a feeling that this is a terrible revenge upon us all for our loss of moral sense, the coarseness of our souls.'

Komsomolskaya Pravda carries a long letter from one of luberi, the tough teenage gangs from the Moscow outskirts who invade the city to beat up the punks and heavy metal fans and the break dancers. 'We find it disgusting to see the chains and badges they wear, their dyed hair, these people who put shame on our country.'

All this was before I had even started to go through my favourite paper, *Sovietskaya Rossiya*. It is getting to the point where if there were another death in the Kremlin, it would take us a while to lift our heads from the papers and notice.

New duty calls
27 April 1987

Mrs Thatcher has certainly started something. The latest symbol of glasnost, the new media openness, is the televised interview of a foreigner.

After Mrs Thatcher's pioneering effort, the visiting American Secretary of State George Shultz was called on to do his bit, although under rather more controlled conditions. As a plump, elderly and not exactly charismatic gentleman, Mr Shultz was hardly expected to wow the Russians in Thatcher-style.

But they took no more chances with the free-wheeling format of the Maggie show, where she charmed, patronized, lectured and floored three Soviet hacks who had never really made up their minds whether this was an interview, a discussion or a party political broadcast on behalf of the Conservative Party.

Mr Shultz was given the straitjacket treatment, a face-to-face with Valentin Zorin, a safe and elderly and rather Richard Dimbleby figure in Soviet broadcasting.

But clearly we are witnessing the birth of a new Soviet tradition. Visiting Western statesmen can now expect a polite grilling before an audience of 180 million, an inevitable part of the Moscow trip, shoe-horned somewhere between the Kremlin talks and the caviar dinner.

But this has another implication. The Soviet interviewers need practice at this new and arcane art. The Soviet tradition in posing questions is hesitant to the point of servility. Witness the first question put to Mikhail Gorbachev in his first ever interview as General Secretary. 'How would you describe the present international situation?' asked the editor of *Pravda*. Not what one would call going for the jugular.

We Western correspondents in Moscow have hitherto been used to a fairly secluded existence in the Soviet media. From time to time, we get denounced as drunks, spies, scandal-mongers and slanderers. In the past, this has been taken in good spirit, with parties being thrown to celebrate when one of us loses his or her virginity in the Soviet press. I recall my former BBC colleague Peter Rush being inordinately proud of one attack in the press in which he was accused of ill-bred behaviour by resting his feet on a low coffee table while waiting for hours between planes at some godforsaken Siberian airport.

Suddenly, we Western slander-merchants are in fashion, invited to write articles for the Soviet press, to give radio and TV interviews, to take part in the rather stilted round table discussions that are being arranged by magazines and academic institutes.

Hitherto, this sort of access to the Soviet media has been largely restricted to the Western journalists who work for the communist press. And many of my capitalist colleagues remain deeply suspicious of the Soviet motives in bringing us, traditional purveyors of bourgeois lies and disinformation, into the glasnost process.

Indeed, some of my colleagues regularly complain at the courtesy of the *Guardian*'s letters page in printing communications from some Soviet spokesman or public relations general, when the Soviet press hardly ever seems to repay the compliment.

But in these TV and radio interviews, we are not being censored. We can say what we want about human rights or Afghanistan or Stalin, and since a gowing number of us speak enough Russian to sustain a lengthy interview, we need not worry about any spin being applied to the translation.

The great difficulty, in a country where the role of the journalist is still officially defined as 'organizer and agitator on behalf of the party', is to stress that we speak for ourselves, not for newspaper or government.

But still, I have found myself in the curious position of having not to defend, but to try to explain, the defence and foreign policies of Mrs Thatcher which I do not personally support. This is partly because I accept her views to be sincere, coherent and reflecting a large body of British and Western opinion.

But it is also because if this new access we have to the Soviet media is to be useful, we have to show that a journalist can take an independent position, neither a spokesman for our own government, nor a fellow-travelling mouthpiece who puts forward the *Pravda* line with a British accent.

Chatting with the Soviet interviewers after the show, I get the impression that this Western tradition and ideal of independent journalism is far more fascinating to them.

But that's the funny thing about television. None of my Soviet friends seem to recall any of the striking things Mrs Thatcher said in her interview. But they can't stop talking about her looks, her hair, her clothes, her voice and her femininity.

Stalinist skeletons: Gorbachev's best-seller on reform

2 November 1987

At 75 kopeks (or 74p) for 272 pages in hardback, the first print-run of 300,000 copies of the steamy new best-seller by Mikhail Gorbachev was going like hot cakes in Moscow yesterday. Hard-bitten journalists queued for their copies and peered over the shoulders of the lucky early buyers to scan the interesting bits. It was like the mass buying of *Lady Chatterley's Lover* when censorship was eased in Britain, except that in Moscow the punters were skimming through for a six-letter word that spelt Stalin. And that obsession with the dark past, with the crimes of a dictator a full generation dead in a seminal book about the future by the most forward-looking of Kremlin leaders, speaks volumes for the awesome grip Stalin still exerts on the Soviet psyche. Perhaps inevitably, Gorbachev says that Stalin's broad strategy of crash industrialization and forced collectivization of agriculture in the 1930s was correct. (Had Gorbachev denounced the principle of collectivization, the reaction of the country's 80 million collectivized farming families of today might have proved alarming.)

'In order to save the gains of the revolution, we had to build, and quickly, a national industrial base with our own internal resources, holding down consumption and reducing it to a minimum. The material burden fell on the people.

'The collectivization of agriculture was a great historic act, the most important social change since 1917. Yet, it proceeded painfully, not without serious excesses and blunders in methods and pace, but further progress for our country would have been impossible without it. If it had not been for collectivization, we could have died from hunger in the war,' he goes on.

Gorbachev strives towards a balanced view of the Soviet past that admits 'dramatic mistakes and tragic events' but yet dares not begin to question the legitimacy of the Revolution and sees Stalin's repressions as an aberration, rather than characteristic of a revolution that became totalitarian in order to survive. But, in the coded phrases in which such debate continues to be conducted even in glasnost Moscow, Gorbachev comes down on the side of de-Stalinization. He praises the 20th Party Congress of 1956, at which Nikita Krushchev first began to reveal the nature of Stalin's repressions.

'At this congress and after it, a vigorous attempt was made to turn the helm of the country's movement, to give an impetus to liberation from the negative moments of socio-political life, engendered by Stalin's personality cult,' he writes. 'And when we look for the roots of today's difficulties and problems in order to comprehend them, to draw lessons for present-day life, we find that they go back deep into the 1930s.'

But the main thrust of the book is to argue that without the full-blooded economic and political reforms of perestroika, the Soviet Union would face a desperate crisis. But the world is now too small and too interdependent to consider the Soviet Union alone: a new relationship between the great powers, based on disarmament and mutual respect, is essential. The problems of the developing world can only be resolved by joint efforts, transferring resources from the arms race to global development.

The book also raises the curtain on this coming week of festivities to celebrate the seventieth anniversary of the 1917 Revolution. And this morning, Mikhail Gorbachev will deliver the most important speech of his career, his official perspective on the great Soviet experiment. It will assess the seventy years of Soviet history in their suffering and in their achievement, and look forward to the nature of the socialism he wishes to develop along more democratic and less authoritarian lines. It is the speech by which Gorbachev's honesty and his sincerity will be judged, by sceptical experts abroad, as well as by his own people, who are terribly torn by the challenge of confronting their own past.

Gorbachev will seek to bridge the vast and dangerous gap between those intellectuals who insist that the truth be told of the sheer scale of Stalin's repressions, and the party bureaucracy who fear that too much frankness could devalue not only the achievements of the past, but undermine the party's authority in the future. Gorbachev, according to sources familiar with his speech, will steer the same cautious line that he adopts in his book, acknowledging the dreadful price Stalin made the Soviet people pay, but arguing that the cost was outweighed by the achievement of ensuring the survival of the Revolution, and the transformation of a backward peasant economy into an industrialized superpower. The speech, which begins in the Kremlin's Palace of Congresses at 10 a.m., will also see a major new foreign policy statement which is likely to focus on the future of Europe, according to senior Central Committee sources.

But the speech takes place under the shadow of the unprecedented public clash over the pace of the reform process in the Soviet leadership between Boris Yeltsin, the Moscow party chief who is perhaps the most outspoken reformer on the Politburo, and the leading conservative figure, Yegor Ligachev. The clash, first reported in the *Guardian* last week, was publicly confirmed at the weekend by Anatoly Lukyanov, a secretary of the Central Committee.

This first public sign of divisions within the Politburo is highly dangerous for Mr Gorbachev, pointing to the anguished nature of the debate within the leadership about how far and how fast perestroika should proceed. With such a divided ruling team, Mr Gorbachev may well feel the need to rein in his own instincts to force the reforming pace, and the text of his speech today will be the more closely scanned as a result.

Duel in the sun

23 November 1987

A few months ago, Roy Medvedev told me that he felt glasnost was for real because there were no longer piles of samizdat literature and underground journals sitting on his desk. The Soviet press itself was reading like samizdat these days, said this learned elderly gentleman, whom only the brain-dead minions of the Brezhnev years could ever have dubbed a dissident. But last week I was present at the birth of a samizdat revival. The journal *Poyedinok*, which can be translated as duel or single combat, appeared nine times at the end of the 1970s and in the early 1980s, until its editors were arrested. Its new, tenth, issue contains 126 pages of typescript, with some sixty copies circulating in Moscow, twelve of them typed originals and the rest carbon copies, in traditional samizdat style.

It begins by reprinting the full text, as well as the secret protocols, of the 1939 Nazi–Soviet non-aggression pact. And although the project was set in train before Joseph Brodsky won his Nobel Prize for Literature, it carries a selection of his later poems, including the haunting 'Now I Depart from Moscow', written in exile. This is a considerable coup in its timing alone, and helps explain the interest the journal has aroused among intellectuals.

It also includes a long extract from Mikhail Voslensky's *Nomenklatura*, a book about the life-style, mind-set and structure of the Soviet party élite. First published in German, and then in English, its author was a history professor at Lumumba University before he fled to the West. He also served as secretary to the Disarmament Commission of the Soviet Academy of Sciences.

The editorial board of the journal is filled with dissident names of the late seventies, some of whom have now rallied to the new independent political clubs. *Poyedinok* also prints the declaration of intent of one of them, 'Democracy and Humanism', which calls for freedom for political prisoners, for removing the ideology from Soviet society and striking out of the Soviet constitution such phrases as 'with the goal of building communism'.

The editorial forward to *Poyedinok* says that 'publication has been renewed in order to help the country return to its past, so tragically disrupted in 1917. Russia could, and should, have chosen a different, bloodless path for her development, and we will endeavour to give our readers the historical and philosophical evidence for this postulate.'

'The journal may be closed, its printing facilities seized, its editorial board arrested, but the word itself cannot be killed,' it continues. 'In the struggle of freedom against tyranny, dissidence against despotism, truth with lies, our journal again appears for the duel.'

This all has a grand ring to it, but I suspect *Poyedinok* is already in danger of being overtaken by the pace of change in Gorbachev's Soviet Union. The poems of Joseph Brodsky, for example, are to be published in the official journal of the Writers Union, *Novy Mir*. *Poyedinok*'s long essay by Ivan Bunin on the poet Mayakovsky claims that by the end of his life he had become 'the lowest and most cynical servant' of the Soviet myth. Strong stuff, except that the latest issue of *Yunost* magazine contains a similar argument from someone who knew Mayakovsky, and spent nearly thirty years in Stalin's camps.

The goals of democracy and humanism, as published in *Poyedinok*, call for amnesties for all prisoners convicted under the notorious articles of the criminal code, for an end to the death penalty, and the publication of banned authors such as Solzhenitsyn, Zamyatin and George Orwell. The Soviet state is lumbering cautiously in the same direction.

It is a frustrating business, being a dissident intellectual in the Soviet Union these days, as one is never entirely sure whether one is with the current or against it. Even the tactics of the secret police have changed. A chum of mine on the editorial board, who has called for demonstrations on behalf of Latvian independence, political prisoners and even Boris Yeltsin, regularly gets arrested by the police just before he is due to leave for the demo. He is held for three hours, the time allowed under Soviet law for a check of documents, before being freed.

Other intellectuals who have rallied to Gorbachev's reforms, even condemn *Poyedinok* as counter-productive, designed to provoke the Soviet system into a backlash against those who push the limited new freedoms too far. But, for the moment, the thrill of late-night typing and clandestine distribution, and the whiff of high-minded conspiracy is back in Gorbachev's Moscow. Time to go and check out the state of Roy Medvedev's desk again.

7

What Living in Moscow is All About

After nearly four years in the city, we can almost claim to be Muscovites. We live in a Soviet apartment block on a street called Serpukhovsky Val, about a mile south of the Kremlin. The street is a pleasant treelined boulevard, on the site of the old city wall. We have two Soviet apartments knocked into one, to give us three bedrooms.

We live much better than the Russians do, because we have access to the two hard-currency supermarkets, where there is usually meat. And when there is not, or when the Chernobyl disaster brought a sense of panic to shopping for groceries, we can import food from Finland. But the biggest difference between us and our Russian friends is that we have visas that allow us to travel to and from the Soviet Union whenever we wish. We also were able to buy a private car, just by signing a cheque. We have a telephone that can dial direct to Britain and the West. And because we pay hard currency, we never have to queue for vodka.

But we endure enough of the hassles and problems of Moscow life, and enjoy enough of the pleasures, to give us that sense of resigned and critical fondness for the place that one gets for any city, anywhere. Over eight million people live in Moscow, and they get born and go to school and fall in love and raise families and are happy or have tragedies just like people do anywhere. Moscow is not that different. For its children, it is a challenge and an adventure. For its lovers, it is a romantic setting. For the Soviet peasantry who come in each day by the millions to shop, it is an El Dorado of consumer goods. And for the elderly and the poor and the harassed, overworked mothers trying to raise kids and run a home and hold down a job, it is a constant nightmare.

It is a great city, because as the capital of a superpower and a multinational state, it has to be. And it can be endearing and fun. But a Big Apple it is not. More of a Big Potato.

Park of delights
4 August 1986

The West knows Gorky Park as the sinister location of the grisly killings in the excellent novel of that name by Martin Cruz Smith. It is time someone redressed the balance, because the Central Park of Culture and Leisure in the Name of Maxim Gorky to give it the full and formal title, embodies a great deal of what is best about Soviet life.

It is in many ways a deeply serious place, where 'culture' has that rather old-fashioned connotation of learning and solemn self-improvement. It is worth looking at the facilities on show last Saturday, for example, which was a theme day dedicated to 'Kosmos – Zemlye I Miru', which translates rather clumsily as 'Space – for the Earth and for Peace'.

This meant a series of lectures and exhibitions and meetings with staff of the Institute of Cosmonautics at each of the four large stages in the vast park complex. There was something called an oral journal, which meant illustrated lectures on how lasers serve men; on space observatories, and on metallurgy in the space age. And there was an exhibition, with guides and lectures, on space exploration in the future.

This was not allowed to monopolize the park facilities. At the central stage, a large open-air theatre, the morning began with poetry readings; then the premiere of a new musical work, and then after the cosmonauts had finished their stint, there was a concert given jointly by musicians from Warsaw and Moscow in the name of Soviet–Polish friendship.

At the musical stage, another of the theatres, there was a

literary concert with excerpts from plays, poetry readings and a brief lecture; then a concert for children, and then the chance to talk with Moscow actors about plans for the forthcoming theatre season, and then the oral journal on space.

At another theatre, called the Stage of the Big Field, workers of the city's cultural department presented a revue entitled *Our Merry Stadium* of songs and jokes and dances, which gave way to a concert of Moscow amateur musicians. This was followed by a brass band concert, and then the evening was devoted to ballroom dancing.

The last of the big theatres, known as Map of the World from its decor, began with a long meeting of the highly popular club of lovers of Moscow history, and in the evening there was a long lecture by eminent doctors who then gave a medical version of *Any Questions*.

While the lectures and concerts went on, the actual leisure of the park proceeded in the manner of such places all over the world. Off-duty soldiers and young bloods showed off to the girls at the shooting gallery, and mothers bought endless tickets for the merry-go-rounds for their children. There were queues at the ice cream stands and happy squeals could be heard from the huge ferris wheel that dominates one bank of the Moscow river just as the Kremlin looms over the other.

There were rowing boats for hire, and rows of solemn drinkers at the Keramika open-air bar who put their 20-kopek pieces into the automat machines to get their half-litre of gassy, yeasty beer. The shashlik stands selling skewers of barbecued meat were doing good business, and miniature tankers came round selling kvass, the refreshing old Russian drink that is made from fermented bread.

People strolled through the formal gardens, and admired the fountains behind the imposing entrance arches, and sat on benches and looked for their children, and flirted and courted and disturbed their neighbours with the rock music coming from their portable tape recorders.

And then if you walked on past all these facilities that the Muscovites know as Gorky Park, and past the embankment where you take the river cruise boats, you come to the loveliest, quietest part of all that is still known by its old, pre-revolutionary name, 'Neskuchniy Sad', or the non-boring garden.

It is quite a surreal place. You climb the steps and stroll through the thick trees to a large sunken garden where all the paths are overgrown by thick weeds. It looks as though gardeners have not been here for years. But they must have been, for the flower beds are ablaze with colour and planted in regular rows. At one corner, an old lady snoozes in her newspaper kiosk. Dominating the garden is an open-air cupola, a monument to the various defences of Moscow from the battles against the Tartars and Poles and French to the Nazi invasion of 1941.

Behind this garden are two children's playgrounds. The first is broken down and dangerous, with splintered climbing frames, collapsed slides, and rusted swings. The other, all carefully done in the old Russian style of rustic wood, is evidently new. The children prefer the dangerous old one. And after all that self-improvement in Gorky Park, who can blame them?

No left turns
1 September 1986

Like most Moscow drivers, I have learned to avoid the Krimsky bridge over the river near the Kremlin on Thursday morning when the Politburo meets. The traffic is held up for miles around as the long black Zil limousines snake out of the narrow road past the general staff HQ, past the Lenin library, and across to the special entrance into the Kremlin.

You get accustomed to this constant presence of motorized privilege. Along the middle of all the main roads runs a special lane, known as the Zil lane because this is reserved for official cars and their motorcades, screaming along the streets at astonishing speeds with blue lights flashing, traffic cops saluting, and all the traffic lights being carefully turned to green.

One of the fastest drives I ever enjoyed in my life came when I went to the airport to meet Neil Kinnock and an official Labour Party delegation which had come for talks with the former leader, Konstantin Chernenko. They were met by a Politburo host in the VIP lounge, and whisked into a Zil motorcade for what is normally a 30-minute drive into the city. I tucked in behind the motorcade and the trip took eleven minutes.

It was one of the few pleasures of Moscow driving; a generally depressing experience made alarming by the weather. In winter, driving on ice is bad enough, but come the spring thaw and you learn that Moscow is the city of potholes, as the ice chews up the road surfaces into great chasms that wreck your suspension and leave the tramlines rising proudly above the wrecked asphalt like little tank-traps.

But like anywhere else in the world, the real menace on the roads comes from other traffic, and the surprise of Moscow is that there is so much of it. In a city with one of the world's finest Metro systems, and reasonable, although much criticized buses, trolley buses, and trams, the age of the private car has come to the Soviet capital.

It is worse in summer, because the 'podsnegniki', or snow-drops (those drivers who put their cars away in garages or under tarpaulins for the long winter), venture out like so many spring flowers when the snow clears. Seasoned Moscow drivers complain about the podsnegniki and their amateurish habits much as people in Britain complain of Sunday drivers.

They have not yet got around to installing parking meters in Moscow, but the day cannot be far away. For the past ten years, the car factories have been turning out over 1,300,000 automobiles a year, most of them the Zhiguli, based on an obsolete Fiat design and turned out on the Italian-designed assembly lines at the vast Toghatti plant on the Volga.

On the whole, the Zhigulis are the private cars. The official cars have a very clear pecking order. There is the Volga, a big saloon that runs off 73-octane petrol that makes up the taxi fleet and the transport for junior officials. Then comes the Chaika, which looks like a Cadillac and is used for official delegations of not quite top rank. The old ones, with the 1950 curves and deep pile carpets, and flower vases are marvellous artefacts, and when you see a cluster of them together you are suddenly transported into a Hollywood movie. Finally come the Zils, sharklike and arrogant.

For obvious reasons, most of the official cars are based in Moscow, but the capital also has a disproportionate share of the private cars. And so do the more affluent republics, like the Baltic states and Georgia.

And with the private cars, and the pride of ownership they inspire, comes a slow but inexorable social revolution. Apart from that minority buying a co-op apartment or a dacha, a car is by far the biggest expenditure a Soviet citizen can expect to make. And keeping the thing running is likely to be his biggest headache. Spare parts are one of the choicest items on the black market, and the private car has probably been the biggest single factor in the surging growth of corruption and the black economy.

The deputy procurator general has just issued a hair-curling statement on the vast industry in black market petrol. In some Moscow service stations, he fumed, the attendants were making so much on the side they did not bother to collect their wages for six months. Even in the last year of strict Gorbachev style discipline, theft of petrol had gone up by 25 per cent. The chairman of the state committee for the fuel industry had been arrested after taking bribes . . . the list of complaints went on and on.

And as I sit in the increasingly common Moscow traffic jams, even when the Politburo is not blocking the roads, I see no end to the social change. The government can try to clamp down on the use of private and off duty official cars as gypsy cabs, and can try to stop the siphoning of state petrol, but once a society has begun its love affair with the automobile, even Opec has yet to find a way to stop it. You might as well try to park in the Zil lane.

Battle of the beetle

10 November 1986

The recent correspondence on cockroaches in the *Guardian* letters page was fascinating, but it lacked the Soviet angle. Any discussion of cockroaches which fails to acknowledge the superiority of the Moscow breed is like talking about snakes while ignoring pythons and cobras. For size, aggression, and tenacity, the Moscow cockroach reigns supreme.

On this subject, I lay claim to a modest expertise. I have flushed the fearsome cockroaches of Mexico City down the plug-hole. I have stomped on the brutes in Benghazi, and jumped on them in Johannesburg, drowned them in Delhi, and been tempted to nuke them in New York.

Elsewhere in the world, the average human stands a fighting chance in hand-to-hand combat with a cockroach. Not in Moscow. The first one we saw when we moved into our 15th-floor apartment on Serpukhovsky Val could have been mistaken for a T-34 tank in brown camouflage. It was conducting obviously hostile manoeuvres across the wooden floor, and with the understandable arrogance of homo sapiens, I tried to crush it flat.

My foot bounced, my knee jarred, the pain stabbed into the base of my skull – and the cockroach strolled placidly on while I stared in disbelief at the damage to the sole of my shoe.

We called on a friendly babushka for help. The babushkas are the grannies, the old ladies who really govern the country and keep it on the straight and narrow. Babushka said mix borax powder with mashed potato, roll it into little balls, drop them underneath and behind the furniture, and await results.

The result was that we could not fight our way into the lavatory for the hordes of cockroaches. A scientific friend explained that the borax stops the cockroach from drinking water, and they eventually die of thirst. But meanwhile they gather wherever they can smell the water they crave. Babushka learned her anti-cockroach lore in an old Russian house with an earth privy. Hence our problem with the lavatory.

There are loyal Russians who will tell you solemnly that

there never used to be cockroaches in Moscow, that the little beasts were first seen at the Kievsky station in 1955, when the first trainload of African students arrived and opened their suitcases for inspection.

This is rubbish. The cockroach is as Russian as borscht. The Russian word for the insect is 'tarakan' and there is an old town called Tarakanov not far north of Moscow.

When I leave Moscow on holiday, I call in the exterminator. You can order this service from the state servicing bureau, but like most Muscovites, I prefer to go private. For a fixed price per square metre, and bottle of vodka thrown in, a kind of Armageddon takes place throughout my apartment. I cannot specify what chemicals are used, but I know all human life is banned from the place for days after the treatment. It costs about £25.

Returning home is like the morning after Waterloo. In the cupboards, along the skirting boards, beneath the chairs, and around the lavatory, the corpses lie in heaps. Some try to escape into the refrigerator, and there are bodies along the rubber seal that keeps the door closed. Others take refuge in the controls of the electric cooker, where they eventually die. My wife knows that to cook a souffle the dial should be turned to two cockroaches, and to roast coffee beans, all the way up to the albino one with the long antennae.

Not only do the tarakans always come back, some of them never leave. Even after the kind of chemical warfare that would turn Caspar Weinberger into a pacifist, some of the corpses eventually twitch, stir themselves as if from a long sleep, and stroll into the kitchen to look for crumbs.

I sometimes wonder whether they might even relish our attempts at extermination as some kind of Darwinian challenge to ensure the survival of their fittest specimens. I know that they can survive extremes of heat and cold, can withstand radiation, and go without food and drink for long periods in a state of suspended animation. And they can hide away in the least likely corners.

I doubt whether the human race has ever sent up a space ship or satellite that did not contain its little creepy-crawly cargo. I see them, antennae twitching, checking out the moon and Venus, and in my worst moments fear that in the endless process of evolution, the function of the human race may be simply to serve as cosmic bus drivers for the real heir to all the ages, the Muscovite tarakan.

A pool in hot water

26 January 1987

Throughout the winter months, a thick cloud of steam hangs over the river bank in central Moscow, swirling and rising like fog in a horror film. It comes from the open-air swimming pool, known as the Moskva, which is usually so warm that a dip is rather like taking a hot bath while the snow drifts on to your head.

The steam means that this is the only swimming pool I know where you see more under water than above it. But the days of the Moskva are now numbered, with art-lovers complaining that the steam is having a terrible effect on the treasures in the nearby Pushkin Museum.

It was never meant to be a swimming pool, anyway. Until the nineteenth century, this low-lying riverside site housed the old Alexeev Monastery. But to commemorate the victory over Napoleon in the war of 1812, they built an enormous and rather ugly church called Khram Khrista Spasitelya, the Cathedral of Christ the Saviour.

The cathedral could house over 10,000 worshippers under its dumpy domes, and old lithographs show its squat dominance over the city's western districts. But in 1932 it was demolished to make way for one of the most grandiose schemes of the Stalin years.

The plan was to build a Palace of Soviets, a formal seat for the country's parliament. The design brief said that it should contain two vast halls, one to seat 20,000 people, and the other to seat a mere 8000. It was to be the biggest building in the world, and to crown it was to be the world's biggest statue, Lenin himself, standing 24 feet high. The entire building was to act as a giant pedestal for the statue of the founder of the Soviet state.

The whole edifice would have been nearly 500 feet high, towering not just over the Kremlin, but over the city itself. It was part of the passion for gigantism that Frank Lloyd Wright denounced at an architects' conference in Moscow in 1937.

They began by building the foundation, rooted on thirty-two pairs of vast steel columns. The concrete took 16 per cent of national production the three years before the war. And they could never get the foundations to hold. River water seeped into them from the side, and salt water seeped up from below, and the sandy river bank soil kept sliding under the monstrous weight.

Whatever the engineers' explanations for their failure, devout Muscovites were quick to point out the evidence of divine displeasure. To this day you can see older people cross themselves whenever they pass the Moskva swimming pool.

The war put an end to it all. They took the steel columns to make into tanks, and the concrete allocated for the foundations was needed for factories and for bunkers on the outskirts of Moscow.

The water seeped in, and the vast hole became a make-shift swimming pool for Moscow children in summer. But the plan still said that the Palace of Soviets should be erected there, and so the local Metro station was named after it.

Krushchev put a brisk stop to it all, building a rather more modest glass and steel palace within the Kremlin walls – which still holds 6000 people – and had the hole turned into the Moskva open-air swimming pool.

But it was all done in rather a hurry. The pool can take many more swimmers than the cloakrooms can accommodate their clothes. According to the chief engineer of the pool, it was always meant to be a temporary structure, and the bulk of water channels and heating systems are now dangerously unsafe.

So the pool is to go, and the debate is now under way to decide what to put in its place. The front-runner seems to be a building that was designed almost ninety years ago by Fyodor Shechtel, perhaps the outstanding Russian architect of his day.

He designed the original Moscow Arts Theatre, where

Stanislavsky put on the premiere of Chekhov's *The Seagull*, and that astonishing fantasy of Russian past and modernist future, the city's Yaroslavl Station.

His plan for a 'peoples' house included a theatre, lecture rooms, restaurants, a library and tea rooms, all under two towers that were meant to echo those on the Kremlin walls.

This column has mentioned before the national craze for restoring and conserving old buildings, but this is the first example I have met of their actually wanting to build one. Given the grim quality of most modern Soviet architecture, I suppose it was only a matter of time. Post-modernism, I fear, is on its way to Moscow.

Joy and grief
16 February 1987

Last week, I was nastily roughed-up while trying to cover a political protest in Moscow's old Arbat. The bruises faded fast, but the sad thing is that I will never again be able to stroll down one of my favourite Moscow streets without thinking of that beating.*

The Arbat has become for me a very real symbol of the changes taking place in the Soviet Union. First, the street itself has been preserved in all its nineteenth-century, higgledy-piggledy charm. Just a hundred yards away there is the 'new

---

* Josef Begun was still in a labour camp when his family and other Jewish dissidents resolved to test Mr Gorbachev's promise of improvement in Soviet human rights policy by demonstrating for his freedom every day for a week in the Arbat, the old shopping street that had been carefully restored as a symbol of Moscow's perestroika. The first two days were calm enough, but then the KGB moved in, beating the demonstrators and the Western press, arresting them, and casting doubt on the sincerity of Gorbachev's reform programme – or more ominously on his degree of control over the KGB.

Arbat', a soulless eight-lane thoroughfare lined with high-rise buildings of dingy grey concrete.

But the old Arbat is pretty much as it was in Tsarist days, except that it has been made into a pedestrian precinct. There are some pretty cafes, including a charming place for children, with miniature furniture, to which unaccompanied adults are not admitted. There is the video salon, where you can hire old Eisenstein movies and modern Russian films.

At the western end of the Arbat is the Foreign Ministry, and at the other end, the Praga restaurant, still one of the best places in Moscow, where diplomats, Soviet officials, and correspondents tend to lunch.

And it remains the artistic centre of Moscow. I forget how many times I have groped up semi-lit staircases to the garrets on top floors where the painters have their studios. They serve you tea and warm glasses of Pepsi as they show off the canvases they know will never be exhibited in public.

Pushkin lived here after his marriage, and so did Lermontov. The Arbat has a magic about it – one of those places that was always at its best just a few years before you got there. It is Moscow's Greenwich Village, its Left Bank, its King's Road, Chelsea. The country's music and literature is stuffed with references to the place. One of my favourite singer-songwriters, Bulat Okudzhava, wrote a very pretty melody for a song that goes:

> Oh Arbat, my Arbat, my homeland is Arbat,
> You're my joys, and source of all my grief.

On a summer evening, when half the city seems to be strolling down its wide paving and there is light in the northern sky until almost midnight, you hear the song hummed from every side.

And then you look at the pretty girls in their stylish dresses, watch the people watching the world go by as they sit in the Arbat cafes, see the crowds come out from the Vakhtangova theatre buzzing with the latest play, you hear laughter and music and you think that Moscow is about to take its place among the great European cities.

You think that at last, after the cultural clampdown and the years of Iron Curtain and thought police, the place has fundamentally changed. I suppose a lot of my optimism about Gorbachev and the future of this country came from evening strolls in the Arbat, from the conversations that went on till dawn in those garrets and other Arbat flats.

I remember standing in the antiquarian bookshop, where I was buying some old prints of Moscow, and getting into a conversation with a middle-aged Russian writer who knew more about the plays of George Bernard Shaw than I will ever remember, and he recited from memory St Joan's last speech as we strolled off down the Arbat to his flat.

I remember walking down the Arbat last autumn with a Soviet diplomat from the Foreign Ministry who was still thrilled by the glimmering of real hope he felt after the Reykjavik summit. He tried to overcome my scepticism at the thought of super-powers voluntarily giving up the nukes that defined their status.

And I enjoyed walking into the little courtyards, going down side streets, and turning into the wide archways that used to take horses and carriages, joining the old men playing chess under the courtyard trees, and the grannies looking after the babies.

But the courtyard I will remember now is the one that leads to the police station, the one down which I saw women being hurled like sacks of potatoes, where my TV colleagues were swatted into the gutter like so many troublesome flies.

I hope the old Arbat can work its seductive magic on me again, that the ugliness of last week was an aberration in a bumpy progress towards a better society. I can hope, but now I understand a little better Okudzhava's song about how the Arbat can also be the source of all one's grief.

Ice and hot

11 May 1987

We went for a picnic at a quiet country lake the other day, stripped off to sunbathe in our swimming costumes and kept our beers cool with chunks of ice we broke from the floes on the lake. That is the speed with which winter has become summer in Moscow.

We had our last flurry of snow just a week before May Day, and yet the May Day weekend saw clear blue skies and a temperature soaring into the seventies, while the ice still lay thick on the Bay of Joys.

I was rubbing sun cream into my wife's back when I saw a picnicking Russian stride out into the icy water, and then climb on to the great shelf of ice that stretched to the far shore. He began to jump up and down on the edge of the ice to make it crack and finally a large block, about half the size of a cricket wicket, broke off and drifted towards the beach.

Heavy enough to remain stable even under the weight of its passenger, the floe bumped on to the sand. It was about 18 inches thick, smooth on top and a mass of long stalactites below, like thousands of icicles fused together.

When the breeze came across the icy bay, you could feel the sudden cooling in the wind even while the sun blazed down. And when one of the river steamers came into view around the trees, you could hear the crashing of the ice as its prow heaved the floes aside.

Spring seems to have come and gone in about four days flat. Just before May Day, the twigs on the bare trees were just beginning to show their hesitant buds. But, as we drove out past the farms towards the Bay of Joys, there was a dusting of fresh green on the fields and the forest had begun to get that rich and fecund smell of summer that makes Russians reach for their knapsacks and go hunting mushrooms.

We are a long way from the sea, but one of the pleasures of Moscow is the summer beaches. Usually, we head for the crowded river bank of Serebrianny Bor, the Silver Woods, a large island in the river to the east of Moscow. Only 30 minutes' drive from the centre of town, most of the big foreign embassies rent a large dacha for skiing parties in winter and sunbathing and barbecue weekends in summer.

You can drive out to the island along Marshal Zhukov Avenue, or take one of the river buses that takes nearly two hours to make the journey from the quay at Gorky Park. Once at the long beaches, you can hire paddle boats or rowing boats for about 60p an hour, and by the end of May the water will be warm enough for swimming.

The Russians like to crowd onto the organized beaches, where there are life-savers and ping-pong tables, and benches where endless rows of chess players sit and brood over their moves and burn their shoulders, while the smell of roasting meat comes from the shashlik barbecues.

But as the river curves lazily northwards, it opens out into a vast lake with endless inlets and bays and promontories which make perfect picnic sites. It means a tedious drive through the northern industrial suburbs of Moscow, and then cross-country through the village of Little Granny, which is how the children translate Babushkino. There are collective farms and woods to pass before we park and walk down through the woods to the low cliff above the lake.

From here we see, to our right, the village cemetery, each family grave fenced off with the newly-painted bright blue railings. Straight ahead, on the next peninsula, is a little jewel of an eighteenth-century church, its onion domes peeking above the trees. The bay itself stretches about a mile wide at this point and, as the summer goes on, the water will thicken with wind-surfers and sailing dinghies.

Down the hill to our left, you can just see the swings and roundabouts of another organized beach, and the open-air cafe and the ice-cream kiosk which, in a week or two, will attract such queues that it will take an hour before you finally get one of the delicious 'Eskimo' cylinders of ice-cream wrapped in chocolate.

The Bay of Joys is vast enough for most people to have found their perfect spot, but if we get bored with it we can head due west to the writers' colony at Peredelkino and have a picnic beside the quiet lake there, where the gardens of the izbas, the old wooden cottages, come down almost to the water's edge, so that the ducks quack in one ear and the chickens cluck in another.

Then there is Secret Lake, out past the privileged Central Committee enclave of Zhukovka, beyond the 'Path of Lenin' collective farm and down through the trees to a chain of large ponds. They are for later in the summer, when the forest earth has dried and the mushrooms are out.

For the next few weeks, as long as the ice is there to cool our beer, we will be heading for the Bay of Joys.

In the steps of the Golden Horde
6 July 1987

I was strolling down Rochdale Street the other day, on my way to the embankment that runs along the Moscow River.

Yes, you read that correctly. There is a Rochdale Street in Moscow, named in honour of the birthplace of the first co-operative shop. It is that part of Moscow known as the Krasnaya Presnaya district, the old red quarter of Tsarist days, where they put up the barricades in the 1905 Revolution before the Tsar's artillery came to blow barricades, district and the textile mills to bits. Not that Rochdale or the Co-op should be proud of the Moscow street. It contains the back end of a dull brick power station, a small and grimy garage with endless queues at the petrol pumps, and some rather down-at-heel apartment blocks.

It runs parallel to the Moscow River, one block to the north, and its main virtue for us Westerners is that it provides a quick short cut to the hard currency shops in the International Hotel, just along the river bank.

One of the great pleasures of Moscow life is the street names. Apart from the City of London, I know of no other capital which boasts a Big Pie Street. And this is no mean alley, but a grand thoroughfare that leads you to the Novodevichi or New Maiden Convent, perhaps the loveliest single building in Moscow, where Krushchev lies buried, where Boris Godunov was proclaimed tsar, and where Peter the Great incarcerated his sister after her failed coup and hanged her supporters outside her window.

Then there is Big Horde Street, named after the route from the Kremlin to the encampment of the Mongol horde. That runs parallel to Big Paddock, where the Mongols kept their horses. Also on the south bank of the river is Piatnitskaya, named after Good Friday, and given the passion of the early Bolsheviks for sweeping away the past, and particularly the religious relics, and re-naming everything in sight, its survival has always been a pleasant surprise.

A friend of mine lives on Pekrovsky Boulevard, which you could translate as the road of the Holy Veil or Holy Shroud. The last time I wrote about the word 'Pokrov' some learned *Guardian* reader wrote in to complain that I had it wrong, and that the lovely church on the River Nerl should be known as the Church of the Intercession. I checked with my orthodox friends at the Danilovskii monastery, and since they translate it as 'holy shroud', that is good enough for me.

But one of the more pleasing (and telling) features of the Gorbachev years has been the ending of this business of re-naming well-loved streets and places. Shortly before Gorbachev came to power, we were informed that Tooth-pullers Boulevard, where the press centre stands, was going to be re-named Shokolov Boulevard, after the author of *And Quiet Flows the Don*. That idea has been quietly shelved, and Tooth-pullers it remains.

Leonid Brezhnev gave his name to the suburb which Muscovites still insist on calling Cherry Tree Borough, and who can blame them? The first brake on this honorific process was applied with the death of the unmourned Konstantin Chernenko, the elderly invalid who briefly preceded Gorbachev. But nobody had ever heard of the small rural settlement that was re-named Chernenko, so rude comment was muted. But now the citizens of the old town of Izhevsk in the Urals, most famous these days for the motorcycles it produces, have successfully petitioned for the old name to be restored. Their home had been re-dubbed Ustinov, after the defence minister.

Now that the precedent has been set, it is interesting to speculate how far it might go. The Urals city of Sverdlovsk is named after one of the old Bolshevik leaders, but it is known to history as Ekaterinburg, the place where the Tsar and his family was massacred in 1918. That might prove a tricky one.

I would not take many bets on the longevity of Brezhnev Borough, but I see little likelihood of Peter the Great's sturdiest testament, the old capital of St Petersburg, ever recovering its old name. It was changed in the last years of the Tsar to Petrograd, as part of the anti-German sentiment during World War One, and although many of the inhabitants still call their city 'Peter', I think the world will know it as Leningrad for a very long time.

That's the thing the Mongol hordes, Tooth-pullers, Lenin and Rochdale all have in common – staying power.

Eyes left
26 October 1987

This November 7 will be my fourth Revolution Day parade in Red Square, and it sounds as if it is going to be a corker. I had grown accustomed to the ritual of it all, the roar from thousands of military throats, the brass bands, the Politburo in their idiosyncratic array of hats walking round the side of Lenin's mausoleum, the jostling of the photographers and the unimaginable noise of the tanks grinding their way past the Kremlin.

My favourite bit was always the generals standing in their open Zil convertibles, right hand at the salute, left hand gripping the special stanchion like grim death as the great cars banked and glided across the slippery cobbles. You always think they are going to slip, and they never do.

But this year being the seventieth anniversary of 1917, we are having a historical pageant with some troops dressed up like the Red Guards who stormed the Winter Palace. There will also be a cavalry detachment of 165 horses from the state stud farm, all trained to withstand the bizarre cacophony of music and shouts and machinery that makes up the Red Square parade. Since the Soviet Army no longer travels on horseflesh, the mounted detachment of the Moscow Police will provide the riders. Then there will be sixteen tachanki, the machine gun carriages of 1917.

This sort of pageantry does not come cheap. The Ministry of

Defence has costed 'documentary research' to get authentic designs at 10,000 roubles. Seven separate ministries were involved in making these things, which cost 5061 roubles each. New versions of the old uniforms have been made, after long research in military museums.

The manning of the parade battalion of the Red Guards posed a problem, according to the parade organizer at the Ministry of Defence, Colonel Belyaev. 'We had to select the troops specially, because the real Red Guards looked much older than our conscripts. They will each be wearing black leather jackets and army caps, with a red ribbon on the chest, a sword and a rifle. The commander will carry a real period mauser,' he recounts.

There will also be detachments dressed in the military uniforms of 1917, with those strange Bolshevik cloth caps that go up to a peak on top, and sailors dressed up like the men who fired the historic guns upon the Winter Palace from the battleship *Aurora*.

The main body of the parade will come, as usual, from the officer cadets of eight élite military academies. There will be sixteen parade detachments, made up of some 2000 marines, paratroops and sailors. They each go through 130 training sessions for the 266 paces they will take across Red Square, at a constant 110 paces a minute. 'They are under great nervous and physical tension. Some of them lose a kilogram in weight during the training,' says Colonel Belyaev.

Each participant goes through a medical check-up on the day before the parade, and one man in each rank carries a stick of smelling salts, just in case.

There are unknown hazards to all this. Apparently the acoustics of Red Square are such that sounds bounce from the Kremlin wall, and it is physically impossible to hear the brass bands coherently if you are standing behind them.

It is all very well for the Politburo up on the mausoleum, or for us journalists and the diplomatic corps on the steps below the Kremlin. But the chaps actually marching hear all sorts of confused and disorienting echoes.

It all sounds as if the city will be more disrupted than usual. The main roads are usually closed off, and we have to obtain special passes for the car windscreens to get past the police roadblocks. On our first November 7 in Moscow, back in 1984, we had been invited to an electoral breakfast at the American Embassy, coffee and Danish pastries, as we heard the results over the radio of Reagan's re-election landslide.

I walked down Kalinin Avenue to Red Square, leaving my wife, then heavily pregnant, to drive back home. It took her three hours, through endless road blocks and diversions to parts of Moscow we have never explored before or since, until she finally got home with the petrol gauge showing empty.

They used to hold military parades on May Day, and also on May 9, the anniversary of the German surrender in 1945. But for a decade now, May Day has been an entirely civilian occasion, and they only hold the Victory Day parades for the big anniversaries, like the fortieth in 1985.

There are even rumours that the new peace policy could put an end to the Red Square military march-pasts altogether, which would be a great blow to small boys of all ages. It would also prevent me from imparting the fascinating news that the red, yellow, blue and white guidelines drawn on Red Square for the tanks and troops take up 500 kilograms of paint.

Reel life

16 November 1987

There is a strange charm about Moscow that I have never been able to pin down, a sense of nostalgia for something I cannot quite remember. But recently a friend of mine, an old American who was first here in the 1930s and again during the war and intermittently since, defined it for me.

'I like this city because it reminds me of war time, when I was young,' he said, and suddenly something clicked into place.

For large amounts of the time here, I feel like an extra in a black-and-white film about the war, or the years just after 1945, Cold War rules and black marketeers and Orson Welles hiding in the ruins of Vienna with that zither music playing the *Third Man* theme.

It is the atmospherics of Moscow that make the city so convincing as a film set. Just round the corner from my office is a booze shop, and every day from late in the morning they start queueing for the 2 p.m. opening, long, patient lines of hunched people in drab clothes huddled against thin snow, like a film clip from *All Our Yesterdays*.

Then there are the shortages, and the last fortnight has seen the worst meat supplies I can remember, even in the free markets and the hard-currency shops. And shortages lead to the grey market, the barter system on which so many people rely, trading Bolshoi tickets or imported shoes for a course of private tuition or a consultation with a leading surgeon.

The wartime British used to describe their American allies as 'overpaid, oversexed and over here', which is how many Muscovites think, with some justification, of the foreigners among them. Like everyone else, I use whisky and vodka and Western cigarettes, which we can get easily enough at hard-currency shops, as an enticing form of hard cash. They ensure plumbing services or scarce tickets or a car repair, just as the wartime Americans used their access to nylon stockings and packets of Lucky Strikes.

There is also that strange sense of celebration that comes with a particular find when you are out shopping, something we have virtually forgotten in the pampered West.

We went out the other day to look at a new market near our house, had to queue behind police barriers before we could get in, but then found some imported Indian coir matting on sale and our entire family went home with a sense of triumph as I carried the prickly rolls back on my shoulder.

One does not take things for granted in Moscow. I got up the other morning and began to make breakfast when the electricity went off again in our part of the city. I shrugged and lit some candles, and then went for my shower to find no hot water. The lift did not work again, and we live on the 15th floor. Once in my office, the secretary telephoned to say she would be late in: the underground had been closed. There was no explanation until the next day's newspaper, which said there had been a fire.

My American friend grumbles that with glasnost it is all starting to change. He used to get a real thrill from the echoes of wartime resistance movements he could encounter in Moscow. It was the way Soviet people adapted to having two identities, one public, when they would spout all the correct phrases and attitudes, and the private face they would shew only in their homes, in the bosom of friends and family, and say what they really felt.

Glasnost has certainly started to change that. There was a very formal lunch at a Western embassy the other day, and one of the leading Soviet economists was talking grandly of the need for drastic price rises to dismantle the swollen system of food subsidy, when his wife broke in. He did not know what he was talking about, she said. Poor people could not afford higher prices, and if he had set foot in an ordinary shop in recent years he would know that he was talking through his hat.

I have heard that sort of thing often enough over pickled herrings and vodka late at night round the kitchen tables, but over lunch at a Nato embassy? That is revolutionary.

And then again, most of my Soviet friends have lost the thrill of clandestine wireless, tuning into the jammed Western broadcasts.

But the mood of Moscow remains. Even though there are break dancers in the pedestrian precincts, jeans and western teeshirts everywhere, the eye is still caught by the unrelenting propaganda. Glory to the Communist Party of the Soviet Union, they say, or USSR, Fortress of Peace, and Communism Will Triumph.

That too is part of the time warp, the wartime sense of propaganda as a standing, living, looming force, surrounding one with the icons of the state, and drumming home its glorious self-image and priorities into the patient citizens who stand in endless queues.

Party line

21 September 1987

Floating high above the Moscow River these days is a huge barrage balloon, of the kind that filled the skies over the Soviet capital during the German blitz of World War Two. In the mass, these things look grey and menacing, but one single balloon ponderously hanging over the city has a rather playful look.

Indeed, this Soviet version of the Goodyear blimp is not intended to block the Moscow skies against any new private pilot flying into Red Square. Instead, it is part of a vast beano organized to entertain the city's population, and very good and colourful it all is.

Over the past few years, I have grown accustomed to all civic festivities being accompanied by the colour red. Red flags, red bunting, red balloons, red fireworks, red armbands so universal that one wondered whether Soviet textile mills were authorized to produce any other colour. But these days, yellows and blues and purples bedeck every bridge and building. The huge street corner placards that used to instruct us all to fulfil the five-year plan now read, 'Honoured Muscovites and Guests, We invite you to share in the city's day of celebration.'

The occasion of all this jollity is the 840th anniversary of the city's foundation in the year 1147 by Long-armed George, or Yuri Dolgoruki as the Russians call him, a petty princeling who built the first riverside wooden stockade on the site of the Kremlin.

The festivities began on Saturday morning with seventy maidens (to represent the seventy years of revolution) dancing in Red Square. By late afternoon, the place was packed with more than 30,000 people, watching the pageants of scenes of the city's history played on three huge separate stages. For those too far back to see, it was all shown on a giant video screen. And at 10 p.m., the specially made bells rang out the opening notes of that pre-Revolutionary song, 'Glory to the Slavic People' for a vast choral singalong while the fireworks blazed out across the sky.

Throughout the weekend, the city was officially instructed to have fun. An estimated two million people thronged the ringroad to watch the parades and pageants. A million flowers were imported into the city to help deck it out and I am told that vodka has been slightly more available than usual. And just outside Red Square the queues for rare boxes of chocolates stretched 200 yards.

In Gorky Park, the carnival began in the afternoon and the bridge from the Metro station looked like a crowd scene from a Fellini movie because of the rule that said entry to the masked ball was restricted to those wearing fancy dress. The biggest queues were at the auto centre in Proletarsky district, where the handmade Zil limousines which Politburo members ride in were available for public inspection and to give rides to children.

In the vast museum park called Vdnkh, the exhibition of economic achievements, there was a craft city where you could buy everything from homemade pies to homemade boots. In the huge square between Gorky Street and the Kremlin there was an unending review called *Moscow I Love You as a Son Does*.

The point is that the city's political leaders are these days enthused by the concept of the quality of life. The process inevitably reminds any Londoner of Ken Livingstone's GLC in its more imaginative moments.

Which brings us to Moscow's version of Our Ken, Comrade Boris Yeltsin, the man who won the all-comers Soviet honesty prize for a famous speech at the last party congress. He launched into a furious criticism of the party bureaucracy, and then said the congress could well ask him why he had not spoken in such blunt terms at the last congress, five years earlier.

'Frankly comrades, I did not have the courage,' he said.

As the new party boss of Moscow, a Politburo member and workaholic who stunned Moscow's party bureaucrats by removing their official limousines and instructing them to use carpools instead, he has brought glasnost to the city streets.

In barely eighteen months, he has improved the city's food supply by inviting collective farms to sell their surplus fruit and veg direct to the public from the backs of lorries.

Generally reckoned to be Gorbachev's most enthusiastic ally in the Politburo, he told the city's party committee this summer that what was needed was open government, brought about and explained to the masses by 'commissars of the perestroika, who listen to the people in order to inspire them'.

Enjoyable and welcome as the Moscow festival has been, it is worth bearing in mind that this, like so many of the Gorbachev reforms, is *dirigiste* rather than democratic. The party has decreed that the people shall enjoy themselves. Start smiling, comrades.

Night life

14 December 1987

In spite of that famous pop song of some thirty years ago midnight in Moscow has never been a whole lot of fun. Indeed the original Russian title of the ditty translates as 'Moscow province evening', which is nearer the mark. Traditionally, this has been a city that goes to sleep early, so that workers can be up bright-eyed and bushy-tailed to do their bit for the five-year plan in the same sort of way that Britain's pub licensing hours were brought in during World War One in an attempt to keep munitions workers sober enough to turn out the shells after lunch.

But the Moscow night is beginning to wake up. This month, the first all-night cinema has opened. Called the Perekop, it is conveniently located near three main rail terminals, and a goodly fraction of the clientele queue at the box office with their suitcases, intent on a cheap night's kip in the warm while waiting for their trains. Perhaps in an attempt to attract film buffs rather than snoozing travellers, the cinema has been showing *The Count of Monte Cristo*, which is a little too noisy and action-packed for nodding off.

The problem is that there is still nothing much to do when you emerge into the freezing winter night. There is one all-night canteen, way out near the Scholkovsksya Metro station, that is said to sell pellmeni, the fatty Russian version of ravioli. There is now a riverboat night club that is open until 5 a.m., but like so many of Moscow's decadent pleasures, including the call-girls, it accepts only hard currency like pounds and dollars and deutschmarks.

Some chemists shops are open across the city and you can at least get out of the cold at the train stations, but the Metro closes down at 1 a.m. There is inevitably another kind of underground, some gay bars and private apartments used as porno cinemas and gambling dens. I once spent a depressing few hours in one of these places, watching people play cards for large amounts of money while drinking neat gin in the Russian style, knocking back the tots in one.

My guide was a sculptor who had a basement workshop, and this place was in another basement of the same block. There were two people I recognized, one from the race track and another, a prosperous young entrepreneur who sells tape cassette copies of Western rock albums, and is now branching out into video.

These are the night people you meet in any big city, but the Soviet capital is now starting to wake up through the Gorbachev economic reforms. More and more factories are going on to a shift system, and this has transformed public transport by night.

There are now 178 bus, 39 trolley and 57 tram routes that are operating night services. Although the idea is being floated, the Metro is unlikely to operate at night because they need the time for maintenance and track repair.

And night work means money. The staff at the Perekop cinema at first resisted the idea of working after the usual 10 p.m. closing time. Their objections were overcome by the new pay scales, which offer them time-and-a-half until midnight, and double pay between midnight and 6 a.m. Suddenly, Moscow cinema workers are clamouring for the right to stay open, and three more cinemas were due to start operating round the clock in November.

They will find competition from Soviet television, which has also recently discovered that life goes on after midnight. It began with a slightly daring talk show called *To Midnight and After*, hosted by a smooth chap called Vladimir Molchanov.

The series began with little fanfare. We came home one night from a party and found our babysitter intent on the scenes of punk aggro in the street that were blaring from the television set. We assumed it was the usual video, until the clip ended and Molchanov began talking to a guest sociologist about youth problems and the generation gap.

The film clip had come from the brilliant Latvian documentary, *Is It Easy to be Young?*, which went from the court trial of rock festival rioters, to punks and drug addicts, and finally to crippled Afghan war veterans and disillusioned young war heroes.

One of the classic symbols of glasnost, this film documentary had started a vast verbal debate in the country that was not seriously taken up in the press. So it was striking to watch television take up the running, and to hear the sociologist quoting with approval a line addressed to the older generation by one of the alienated young people in the film, 'We are what you have made us.'

A few weeks ago, I would have been amazed to read a letter in *Komsoloskaya Pravda*, the party youth paper, calling for condoms to be put on sale widely through vending machines. Now it seems old hat. We heard it first on late-night radio.

The old storey
11 January 1988

Moscow is a city of palaces. They may no longer be used as such, but the stately homes of the old aristocratic families still define the character of its architecture, and provide a sense of continuity with the pre-Revolutionary past.

This first really struck me when some long detour took me down a side street and upon a marvellous old palace whose nameplate proclaimed it to be the Academy of Agricultural Sciences. 'That's the Yusupov place,' observed my companion, like so many Muscovites an amateur historian of the city. The only Prince Yusupov I knew anything about was Felix, the Oxford graduate who had gone home to St Petersburg just before World War One and taken part in the conspiracy to murder Rasputin, the mad monk.

But this palace had originally been given to the Yusupovs by Peter the Great, to the second in command of his army. Subsequent Yusupovs built the great palace of Archangelskoye outside Moscow where Pushkin often stayed, and dedicated his poem 'To a Nobleman' to his host. Most of these grand old buildings claim some link with Pushkin. He used to play cards at the English club on Gorky Street, which is these days the Museum of the Revolution. The English took the rather fine red ochre and single-storey palace from Duchess Razumovskaya.

But half the old buildings in Moscow have housed the English Club at some point or another. The street which is these days named after Kirov, the man whose assassination in 1934 launched Stalin's purges, used to be called Visnitzkaya, or Butcher's Street. By grisly irony it leads to the famous Lubyanka, and in the old days, centuries before the secret police established their headquarters there, this was the site of the English court, where the British merchants were licensed to stay and to trade the goods they brought round through the Arctic Ocean and White Sea and up the river system to Moscow.

In the eighteenth century, the English Club was established in a palace originally owned by Prince Gagarin, who was governor of Siberia and hanged by Peter the Great for corruption. This Gagarin is not thought to be any relation of the first man in space, but you never know. Then the club moved in 1802 to a mansion requisitioned during Napoleon's occupation of the city in 1812 by the French Army *intendant* who was to become better known as the novelist Stendahl.

It then became a hospital, which it is to this day. The English Club, meanwhile, had moved to a palace owned by Count Benckendorff, the chief of police and a man who played a shadowy part in the duel which was to kill Pushkin, and those parts of the historic map of Moscow which are not defined by the travels of the English Club are marked by Alexander Pushkin. He is even linked to the big grocery store, Gastronom Number One on Gorky Street.

For the two decades before the revolution, this was the city's famous foodstore called Yeliseyev's, and most Muscovites still call it by that name to this day. It was celebrated not just for its food, but for its decor, the mirrored ceilings and stuccoed walls, the luxurious surroundings for the displays of fruits and cheeses. But Yeliseyev's was an up-market grocery for less than twenty years before the Revolution.

The Petersburg merchant Yeliseyev bought the building in 1898 from the liberal aristo and art patron Zenaida Volkonskaya. She was the descendant of Prince Sergei Volkonsky, who gained a hero's reputation in the Napoleonic wars, and then took a leading part in the Decembrists' uprising against Tsarist absolutism in 1825. He was condemned to death for his part in the rising, but the sentence was commuted to twenty years hard labour in the Nerchinsky mines in Siberia, and the desperate trek of his wife Princess Maria to join him in penal servitude is one of the great epics of love and loyalty and politics. It also inspired Nekrasov's poem 'Russian Women'. Princess Maria set out on her journey from the house which became Yeliseyev's, and it was there that Pushkin presented to her his great poem of support to the revolutionaries, 'Message to Siberia'.

As the nineteenth century went on, the Volkonsky Palace became known as the house of the opposition, the centre of the *bien-pensant* liberal aristocracy, one of the factors that was to give nineteenth-century Russian progressive thought its shape and identity. It is a sobering experience to muse on the house's glorious history when you stand in line to buy some Soviet-style Roquefort cheese, and look at today's drab display of teas and biscuits. But this kind of history through architecture is one of the great pursuits of the modern Russian intelligentsia, as they try to rediscover their national history and culture after so much of it was dragooned into Soviet shape. As a city of palaces, Moscow is also a city of memories.

8
Foreigners

Just across Red Square from the Kremlin, where the GUM department store now stands, is a part of the city which in the Middle Ages was surrounded with walls and named Kitaigorod, which translates as Chinatown. This has nothing to do with the Mongol invader and the Tartar yoke. The name is said to stem from the way in which trade used to mean the silk route from China, because the sealed ghetto of Kitaigorod, under the guns of the Kremlin, was reserved for foreign merchants.

The location may have changed, but the principle of geographically separating us dangerous and subversive foreigners from our Russian hosts lives on to this day. Apart from the embassy compounds, there are a score of apartment blocks scattered around the city, each surrounded with wire fences and with police checkpoints at the gates. And all of us, from Czech diplomats to Afghan security men to American businessmen to British journalists and Angolan military attachés, have to live in them. There is no choice about this. We are all assigned our apartments by an anonymous government agency, and are all lumped together as dangerous foreigners, and treated as a rather contagious virus.

I am not sure whether the policy behind this is mainly to spare us the rigours of Soviet life, or spare the Russians from our wicked foreign ways. Probably both. But it has the inevitable consequence of throwing us foreigners together. The lack of decent Soviet restaurants or night clubs meant that the foreigners have traditionally socialized among themselves.

And thus Moscow is one of the most relentlessly social of postings for any foreigner. Quite apart from home entertaining there are embassy cocktails and formal lunch and dinner parties and buffet-dances. Even though I tried to spend as much time as possible with Russian friends, I found that a black tie and dinner jacket were an essential part of my Moscow wardrobe. In effect, this attempt to quarantine the foreigners turned out to be yet another example of the remarkable Soviet propensity for shooting themselves in the foot, because the more the rest of the world had to socialize together, the more we complained and gossiped and built a solidarity against our hosts.

There were more than enough of us to build a self-sufficient community, over 2500 accredited diplomats, some 350 journalists and rather fewer businessmen; together with families and support staff, not far short of 20,000 people. Throw in the exchange teachers and students and the growing tide of tourists, and the numbers of foreigners roaming Moscow at any given time must have been the despair of the KGB.

Over the years, and collectively, we probably had more effect on Soviet life than any number of treaties and state visits, simply by living there with our Western clothes and cars and attitudes. It all seeped through, thanks to the highly efficient black market which swiftly saw most Muscovites proudly sporting a pair of Levis jeans, and a striking proportion of them smoking Marlboro cigarettes and drinking Scotch whisky. Western students quickly learned how to extend their grants by judicious trading of stereo tape decks and cassettes of rock music. And as personal computers and videos became commonplace consumer goods in the West, they too began to spill over into Moscow, a cultural invasion that most of the locals were only too pleased to welcome. So it would be unfair to ignore the role of the foreigners in Moscow life. And this selection may also give some insight into the curiously constrained way that the Western press went about bringing the news from the Soviet capital.

Voices in the dark

15 September 1986

The phone rings in the *Guardian* Moscow office at Gruzinsky Pereulok and the voice says in excitable Russian that its owner has just flown in from Georgia or Latvia or Siberia and wants to see me again and where can we meet?

In the old days, the days before Nick Daniloff found himself in Moscow's Lefortovo prison after attending such a meeting, I would have gone as soon as possible, looking forward to renewing an acquaintance and hearing some gossip and sharing a convivial meal.

These days, like all of my colleagues in the Western press in Moscow, I will be thinking twice, trying to remember the exact circumstance in which I met the caller. And I will be nagged by the seed of doubt and mistrust that the Daniloff affair has sown in all our minds.

For the moment, most of us are operating under what we call Cold War rules. When we go to meet Soviet contacts, we take a colleague along, just in case. We let wives and friends know where we are going, and when we should get back. We shy away from the usual casual meeting places outside Metro stations and on favourite boulevards and try to arrange appointments in our offices, even as we know that walls have ears and phones have tape recorders.

The problem is that over the years, a pattern of working has been forced on the Western press in Moscow that would arouse the suspicions of even the sleepiest KGB men.

Because of our concern for our Russian friends and contacts, we are discreet in our meetings. When we go to their homes, we go by Metro, rather than in our cars with their glaringly distinctive number plates. When we invite them to our homes, which are invariably surrounded by wire fences and floodlights with a police guard on the gate, we drive them fast up to the door and rush them inside, to spare them the problems that can come from a police check on their documents.

We get phone calls that begin 'Do you recognize my voice?' and go on to say that Sasha has been arrested, or that Lev has lost his job because he applied for a visa, or that Marina made the trek to the prison but was unable to see our friend.

These days, those dissident stories and contacts make up only a fraction of a journalist's work in Moscow. But ironically, the growing access that we are getting to Soviet officials and academics and the well-informed people in think-tanks has imposed another kind of caution.

If you are lucky enough to get the home phone number of one of these people, and are on good enough terms to talk frankly, rather than hear an instant replay of that day's *Pravda* editorial, the etiquette is that you phone from a public call box. Or you meet in private homes or over lunch, or take a stroll together.

It is not that there are secrets being conveyed, but we are still living in the shadow of an older, grimmer Soviet security system, when even to think aloud about policy options in front of a foreign journalist was to risk one's head.

At least, we thought, it was only the shadow of the bad old days, but the arrest of Daniloff means that the old nightmares are still with us. This is bad news for us journalists, but in the long run rather worse news for the Soviet system.

The growing openness and frankness that was developing between us and the Soviet policy-making establishment in the eighteen months since Gorbachev came to power improved our insights into the way the system worked, and probably gave the Soviet Union a better international image than it has enjoyed for years.

If that process comes to a halt after the Daniloff affair, the Moscow journalism will be back to square one, translating the Soviet press and reporting the press conferences. In short, acting simply as conveyors for the information Moscow wishes to make known.

This, of course, may be what the KGB's heavy mob intended. There are people here who loathe the way the growing number of Western correspondents try to extend the flimsy potential of the Helsinki accords and the Soviet PR machine slowly accepts that its own increasing slickness starts to make Moscow more and more of an international news centre like any other.

We have yet to learn, and it may prove a painful process for some of us, whether the Daniloff case was a strange aberration, or the start of a new policy. For the moment, I believe it was the former, but, like every Western reporter here, I am now living under Cold War rules.

Ticket to ride

17 November 1986

When we flew back to the Soviet Union recently and unpacked our bags, I made a list of items we had brought in for friends and contacts. This column has already made mention of the peculiar deficiencies of the Soviet system which leads us to bring in large stocks of Tampax and condoms for our chums, so we need not go into that.

The list begins with several pairs of women's tights, not just the plain sort but the jazzy, patterned numbers. Then there are the cosmetics, perfume and after-shave and the little trays of assorted eye make-up. We used to bring in the cheap digital watches and electronic calculators you can buy in the West for less than a fiver, but the Russians now make their own. Most popular now are clothes with designer labels like Lacoste shirts and Dior stockings.

Felt-tip pens were on the list and at this time of the year so are Western calendars with lavish photos. Because a lot of our friends are involved in music and drama, there are always new rock tape cassettes and the odd rock video that friends come to us to watch.

The magazines make up a huge stock. There are the rock music weeklies, and the theatre and arts magazines, and the thick copies of *Vogue* and *Harpers and Queen* that I always think are going to send us overweight. There are the personal computer magazines for the buffs, a yachting magazine for a keen sailor and the literary reviews for an academic friend.

Then there are the books. Not just all the latest paperbacks and some Mills and Boon and astrology books for my secretary, but the books in Russian. At Foyles or Collets in London you can buy Soviet books that are almost unobtainable in Moscow. Usually I can pick up copies of rare books like collections of Akhmatova's poetry or even Bulgakov's *Master and Margarita* in the hard currency shops in the big Moscow hotels. But some books are still so rare here you have to buy the exported ones and re-import them. Crazy, but there we are.

Back to our list from the suitcases. There are the novelty items like the flowered notebooks and erasers and pencil sharpeners in bizarre designs. There are jeans and cheap plastic shoes in day-glo colours and silk ties for men. There are strangely-shaped sunglasses and punk ear-rings, plastic aprons for cooks, pots of French herbs and bottles of Chinese sauces, English tea and butane cigarette lighters.

All this makes me sound like some eighteenth-century slaver heading for West Africa. It is not quite like that.

The Soviet Union remains a gift culture. When we go to visit friends or they come to us, gifts are exchanged. And we are often terribly embarrassed by the generosity of our hosts and guests. One of our closest friends, a senior official, brought us a beautifully enamelled samovar from the old city of Tver, and another time, a bottle of rare and wonderful Admiralty V vodka.

Our artist friends give us paintings and authors give us books they have written, signed with that prolix formality which is characteristic of Russian letters. Musicians bring tapes of their music or records, if established enough. And there is always a small gift for our children, a wooden toy or an illustrated book.

When friends arrive from Georgia or the south, they call at the markets before they board the plane or train and buy fresh fruits and local spices. They bring the good Georgian and Azerbaijan cognacs that are hard to find in Moscow. From Lake Baikal they bring Siberian honey or even the delicious fat and red potatoes you find only in Irkutsk.

And they too bring books that are unobtainable in Moscow. The local printing house in Irkutsk produces marvellous books of memoirs of the Decembrists who were exiled there in the early nineteenth century, and the novels of the local author Valentin Rasputin, who remains loyal to the Irkutsk publishers even though he is one of the outstanding novelists of the Soviet Union.

Friends from the Baltic republics bring us that strange local drink called Riga Balsam, or tapes of Latvian and Estonian rock musicians that we never hear in Moscow. The gift culture is an astonishing process of cross-fertilization, because it involves not only us foreigners who live here but the far-flung Soviet citizens themselves.

In its own way, it probably helps to bring this vast continent of a country together almost as efficiently and certainly more pleasantly, than the national TV network, and helps to compensate for the deficiencies and lack of imagination of the state retail system.

Have a nice day

23 March 1987

The programme for Mrs Thatcher's Moscow visit revolves around the meeting in the Kremlin, but there will be some time for sight-seeing, so let me suggest a tour of the Moscow I think she ought to see.

We would breakfast at the new co-op restaurant on Kropotkinskaya Street, where the staff's income depends entirely on their takings. Some apple juice and coffee, fried eggs and ham and fresh-baked French bread in clean and cheerful surroundings will cost less than £2, and I think her presence might help us to jump the usual queue.

Then off down to Brezhnev Borough, which Muscovites still call Cherry Blossom, for the farmers' free market. A glance at the suckling pigs and rabbits and vast lumps of the fat lard and fresh honey and sour cream, and we head for the corner where they sell the painted Easter eggs and wait for Misha. He will sidle up, and bring from his pockets some exquisitely painted wooden eggs, with scenes of old churches and the sign XB for 'Christ is risen', and we will bargain him down to 15 roubles for two.

Then, this being a weekend, we would drive down to Bitza Park, and stroll through the trees and past the children's playground of miniature old Russian wooden houses, and to the path where the open air art market still flourishes. A water colour of the loveliest building in Russia, the Church of the Holy Veil on the River Nerl, will cost about £30 and will look very well in Dungovernin' when she comes to decorate the retirement home. We would drive back past one of the petrol stations, and observe the kind of queue we only see in the West when Opec sends the prices surging, and the speculators asking the drivers if they need any spare tyres, batteries, windscreen wipers or other spare parts that are hard to find.

Then a loop to the Andronnikov Monastery to look at the collection of Andrei Rublev icons. He was a monk here, and is buried somewhere in the monastery grounds, and his greatest work, *Cathedral of the Saviour*, should tell her more about Russian spirituality than any number of briefings.

Time for lunch, and we would have to make a special appeal to Anatoly Krapivsky because he does not believe in queue-jumping, but his Stolyshniki restaurant in the basement of the old palace that was French Cavalry HQ in 1812 is one of my favourite places. For a fiver, we get a set lunch of a little caviar and smoked fish and salad, and then a bowl of beef stewed with raisins and vegetables. On the stroke of 2 p.m., we will be allowed to share a bottle of the sweet Russian champagne.

We would then stroll down Pushkin Street into the back of the Bolshoi and attend some rehearsals, turn left up the hill to Detski Mir toy store and take a look at the KGB building before crossing the road and going through the old red brick wall that is all that remains of Kitaigorod, the old Chinatown where foreign merchants used to live under the guns of the Kremlin. We would go quickly through the arcades of the store, pausing only for a chocolate roll ice cream at the fountain, and then into Red Square, past St Basil's and into my favourite quarter, the Zamoskvorechya, the city's Left Bank.

I would tell her of the novels of Yuri Bondarev, which always include a scene set here, walk over the hump-back bridges and into the courtyards where you can still find the izbas, the wooden cottages, amid the eighteenth- and nineteenth-century town houses, and cross Good Friday Street to the Church of the Assumption to hear the priests chanting as the women come and go.

The car would magically have re-appeared to take us to the bustle around the Zil plant at Avtozavodskaya, and into the local exhibition hall to see the latest constructivist art show.

We should have time to bowl along Enthusiasts' Highway to the Church of the Old Believers, a dark and solemn place, where she can inspect the little free enterprise factory where they make candles from beeswax and tiny brass plaques of the saints, a useful source of income.

Then back to the centre, to the Estrada Theatre on the riverbank to see a Russian variety show rather than the usual Bolshoi evening. We will eat caviar canapés at the buffet before going on to the crowded and art-crammed flat of an English-speaking novelist friend who lives off the Arbat, for supper and gossip and vodka and glasses of tea until almost dawn.

The last stop is almost at Moscow Airport, a sombre memorial of three giant steel tank-traps, ten miles from the Kremlin, and the nearest point the German panzers reached in 1941. Then I think she would be ready for Mr Gorbachev.

Sad Sam's happy days
18 May 1987

To any foreigner who has ever spent time in Moscow, the words Sad Sam will never mean a lugubrious gentleman named Samuel, but a down-at-heel apartment block on that section of the Moscow ring road known as Sadovaya Samotyochnaya, which means 'the garden waterflow'. Sad Sam is the inevitable contraction, and it is celebrated in Moscow legend because this nine-storey block, built by German POW's after the war, is probably the greatest concentration of gossip, rumour and intrigue east of the Berlin Wall.

All Westerners in Moscow, diplomats and journalists and businessmen alike, live in a handful of apartment houses scattered across the city. Each compound is surrounded by a fence with 24-hour police guards. But Sad Sam was one of the first where they decanted the Western press.

It contains the offices and the homes of the Reuters and French press agencies, the BBC, both the *New York* and *Los Angeles Times*, the *Daily Telegraph*, the *Christian Science Monitor*, CBS-TV and a Japanese news agency. It also houses the *Financial Times*, several British military attachés and the British Embassy's press spokesman.

When the Russians go on about 'information imperialism' (and they often do), I suppose they have in mind the envy of those other Nato press attachés who suspect that the (British) lion's share of those 'Western diplomats believe' quotes that you read in the world press are coming from the popular and convivial Sad Sam neighbour, the Maclaren of Maclaren, the British Embassy spokesman.

Sad Sam is the kind of place that makes you wish you had trained as a social psychologist. There are theses begging to be written on the herd instincts of journalists, on the interaction of press and diplomats, on the role of the nanny as gossip, and on the way the various national groups of French and British and American and Japanese go about their journalism.

But the greatest fun of all would be to write the scripts of the Sad Sam soap opera, which would wipe the ratings floor with *Dallas* or *Dynasty*. The latest episode would focus the outbreak of born-again fundamentalist Christianity among the nannies. This is currently the talk of the Moscow cocktail circuit, with dark accounts of their hapless employers finding tiny tracts reading, 'Lord preserve me from my godless employers' stuffed into their carpet slippers. They do tend to go around asking if one has had a personal experience of Jesus, and it is disconcerting to hear one's five-year-old daughter solemnly assure you that God does not love all children, but only the ones who have been saved.

There is even a bizarre view in the American Embassy that this outbreak of Christian chastity among the nannies helped turn the frustrated Embassy's US marine guards towards the dangerous wiles of the KGB's Mata Haris.

Then there are the parties, which Sad Sam throws better than anywhere else. We recently had a recreation of Berlin in the Twenties for a *Cabaret*-style evening as a farewell party for one popular correspondent. And the Sad Sam summer soirée is the high point of the Westerners' social year.

It starts with Pimms and champagne in the various apartments, and then down to the courtyard for a vast barbecue with drinks and dancing. The enterprising British Airways local manager flies in British bangers and provides the cutlery and paper plates, and it goes on all night, with Moscow's best jazz band playing through till the mass bacon and egg breakfast at dawn. If the Politburo ever wants to mount a quiet coup, it should choose the Sad Sam party night, because they could drive the entire tank corps into the Kremlin and not a journalist or diplomat would be around to notice.

But Sad Sam's primacy is coming under threat. The impact of Gorbachev and glasnost has inspired that half of the world's press who had no Moscow bureau suddenly to apply for accreditation. So a new apartment block near the Taganka Theatre is now filling with the *Irish Times* and ITN TV news and the *Independent* and Canadian and Australian newspapers, and the place looks set to rival Sad Sam as a rumour mill.

It has some way to go. The average Sad Sam dinner party will have the KGB chief sacked, half the Politburo in exile and Gorbachev divorcing Raisa before you finish the soup.

Under Eastern eyes

31 August 1987

Strange how easy it is to get accustomed to things, and to cease to notice them. But the other day I made a point of noting how many times in a Moscow day I was stopped and asked for my documents, or went through a police checkpoint.

It began after breakfast when I drove out of the foreigners-only compound where we live. The police box on the gate (manned round the clock) checked me out and picked up the phone to report that I had gone. I drove through central

Moscow to my office, where there is another permanent police post, and he checked me in. When I take my two-year-old daughter to her play group in a room by the British Commercial Office, there is another police checkpoint there. This may seem superfluous, but the vigilance of Soviet security, confronted with dangerous foreign agents using the disguise of a toddler accomplice, should never be underestimated.

From my office, I drive to the Press Centre for a press conference. This time my Soviet Press Card is scrutinized before the way is cleared. On the way back, because it included a more than usually virulent attack on the White House, I call in at the US Embassy to see if they have a comment, and again, show my documents to the police on guard before I can go in.

Then comes shopping. One of the main hard-currency food stores (and thus one of the few places in Moscow where there is never a meat shortage and you do not have to queue for two hours for a bottle of vodka) is located in the International Hotel. Documents, please.

Invited to lunch at an Asian embassy, and another flash of the documents to get in. On the way back to my office, I call in for an interview at one of the foreign policy think-tanks, and having told the doorman I have an appointment, he has to see my Press Card, and take a note of the name and number before he calls up to see whether I can be allowed to proceed.

If I am doing a radio piece, there is another police check at the entrance to the Moscow version of the BBC, and a Soviet broadcasting official has to come down to escort me through the door, both entering and leaving.

Again, if there is a cocktail party at the British (or indeed, any other) Embassy, there is more dithering with documents at the gate. And when I finally head for home, there will be the little aluminium police box at the entrance to my compound to check me in for the night.

One gets used to all this very quickly, and the absurdity of it came home to me only recently when I was in East Berlin for the Warsaw Pact summit. I took the opportunity to go through Checkpoint Charlie into West Berlin, and that monstrous symbol of the Cold War unhinged something in my brain. Perhaps it was the relative lack of contrast between the taste of the beer, the dialects of the Berliners, the look of the two showcases on either side of the Wall. Perhaps it was just the overwhelming contradiction between reporting another Gorbachev speech on the need to build trust in 'Europe, our common home', and the nasty, brutish fact of a system that still feels the need to wall its people in.

Indeed, when I had the temerity to ask a Soviet spokesman at a press conference in Berlin whether he could foresee a day when the Wall might come down, he replied that it was 'a symbol of the stupidity of the leaders of the three Western powers who were responsible for its being built'.

The next day, another British journalist asked a similar question, noting that the Queen had on her visit to West Berlin expressed a hope that the Wall might come down. He was given a similar brusque reply, along with a curt aside about 'provocative British journalists and their campaign on this issue'.

And that got me thinking about the little walls around the foreigners' homes and offices in Moscow, the document check before our Soviet guests can be invited inside, the ubiquity of checkpoints as a characteristic of the system.

And it reminded me of the great thunderstorm that hit Moscow in the summer of 1984, when the skies turned black and a great wind gusted, and the police box outside the biggest of the foreigners' ghettos was blown over and over against the parked cars with a militiaman still inside. And as he climbed slowly from the wreckage, a great shout came from every balcony, as blacks and Asians, Nato and neutral, diplomats, journalists and businessmen and their families took up the chant: 'Do it again, God.'

9
Consuming

In spite of the shortages and the queues and the deep inefficiencies of the Soviet system, 280 million people are living through what they see as an unprecedented consumer boom. There may not be much meat, and fresh fruit and vegetables may be sparse in winter, but nobody goes hungry. And almost every household now owns a TV set, and most have a refrigerator and a washing machine, and even the prospect of eventually owning a private car is no longer out of reach. At current levels of production of about 1.5 million cars a year, it will take the industry over fifty years to provide a car for every household. But with 250,000 million roubles sitting in the state savings banks, or almost 1000 roubles for every man, woman and child in the country, it is hardly the consumers' fault that this is not quite a motorized society. They can afford it. The fault rests with the producers, and that means with the state, which has decided on other priorities.

Whatever the state may think, the Russians have a proverb 'Krasivo zhit' – ne zapretish', which means that it is not forbidden to live well. And most of them are conscious that they are living better than the Russian people ever did before, and are reasonably grateful to the state and system which has provided their prosperity.

These things are relative. On our first trip back to the West, my daughter Kate was three. As we walked through customs into the shopping arcades of London's Heathrow airport, we all stopped in our tracks, stunned by culture shock. Kate was first to recover, saying, 'Look – there are things in the shop you can buy'.

But there are things in the Russian shops too, and the longer we spent there, and the more friends helped us to crack the secret codes of the Soviet retail and distribution system, the more fun we had out of shopping, and learning how to consume as the comrades do. We never leave home without a wallet full of cash and an 'avoska', or just-in-case, string bag in the pocket – just in case we see something worth queueing for. And when we see a real find, like the multi-coloured dressing gowns from Uzbekistan in a clothes shop, or big cushions, or a set of dolls' furniture or the Valenki felt boots, you let your friends know, or even buy some for them too.

Soviet shopping is a strange mixture of wartime rationing and consumer boom. It is still frustrating and tiresome and ill-organized so that there are curious moments of triumph when you actually find something you wanted. It is infuriating that the quality of goods is so bad that even when you get what you want, you may have to take it back two and three times to get it to work. And at the same time, the new cooperative (which means a kind of private enterprise) restaurants and up-market shops are opening.

There is the tantalizing promise of a better system just starting to happen, even as we all still curse the rigidities and failings of the old one.

Shopping after Chernobyl
16 June 1986

The withered old crone in a floral headscarf gazed blankly at us across the counter piled high with succulent red strawberries. They glistened in the thin light of the covered market as we asked her where they had been grown. 'Krasnodar,' she muttered.

Her neighbour, an ebullient young Georgian with a thick stubble chuckled villainously and said, 'Tell them the truth, Granny. They're from Chernobyl.'

Across the aisle, a Japanese family was waving a portable Geiger counter over some plump tomatoes. In the Moscow free markets, the Japanese are called the 'tiki-tiki' these days from the characteristic clicking of the little radiation monitors they carry.

Until Chernobyl, the free markets were one of the great pleasures of living in Moscow. At the big central market, beside the old circus, you could smell the flowers as you pushed through the doors from the street, and then you walked into a blaze of colour.

Past the flowers, you realized anew each time that the Soviet Union was a vast continent of a country, so big that something was always in season somewhere. There were the huge apples from Alma-Ata near the Chinese frontier, the little sweet tomatoes from the Black Sea coast, the pomegranates from Georgia, and the heaped mountains of raw honey and fresh thick cream and the pickled garlic from the collective farms around Moscow.

It is the kind of sight to stun any tourist into total silence. Our preconceptions about the Soviet Union do not prepare us for this sudden evidence of plenty, where the rationing works by the good old capitalist method of price. In winter the tomatoes are £20 a kilo and a single cucumber can cost £8. And you pay the money readily for the sudden delight of crunching something fresh and green after weeks of potatoes and cabbage.

Our own favourite market is a relatively new building of aggressive concrete, looking a bit like a flying saucer. It is known as the Cherry Tree Market, after the traditional name of this suburb of Moscow, now called Brezhnev Borough.

We like the Cheremyshinski market because of the long lines of suckling pigs and the arrays of fresh-skinned rabbits of all sizes. 'Listen, comrade, buy the mum and dad and I'll throw in the two little ones for free,' they say.

There was the day we haggled to buy half a cow, to take it home and carve it up ourselves and put the joints in the freezer. That was when we got to know Misha the cripple, the uncrowned king of the market, who could get anything at a price. He hobbled arrogantly into the crowd of stall-holders around us as we poked and punched at the various carcasses, informed us that the price per kilo was fixed, but the weight was subject to negotiation, and winked hugely. After the crackdown on the black marketeers, Misha has been lying low lately.

This is the market where the little old men pull beautifully-painted wooden eggs from the pockets of their old army greatcoats and show you the half-forbidden religious images they have painstakingly inscribed.

The chickens here taste the way chickens do in dreams of childhood, and there is one stall where you can buy old medicine bottles filled with adjika, the fiery tomato purée they make down in Georgia. For a feast, buy a chicken and some adjika and some salads, and then go to the back door of the Pitsunda restaurant and get some fresh, hot lavash, the flat Georgian bread.

They know our children in the market, and Katie skips down the aisles to the women who call her Katyusha and give her tastes of honey and cream. And when they weigh vegetables, they usually throw in an extra one 'for the baby'.

But the markets now are sombre places. Prices have never been so low, as the foreigners stay away and even the Russians are being cautious. The stalls are filled with cherries and strawberries, and the sellers point to the labels on the boxes that say they come from Bulgaria, or swear that they were grown in the Moscow region.

The newspapers say that everything is being tested before being allowed on sale, and the police check the passports of the sellers to see if they come from the 'special zones'. But then we have all seen the discreet transactions that take place behind the market or near the Kievsky station where the Moscow salesmen buy boxes of produce, no questions asked.

The free markets have been little oases of colourful, carefree capitalism in the Soviet Union, and the entrepreneurial instinct is not going to be crushed by a little thing like radiation. So for months to come, one of the delights of living in Moscow will have to be forgone.

Empire of plenty
30 June 1986

For the average Muscovite, the Soviet empire means pineapples from Vietnam and little red potatoes from Cuba – sweet as nuts and these days guaranteed radiation-free. It means the Polish frozen-food shop and Bulgarian jams, Hungarian salami and Czech beer. In spite of the Hungarian-built Ikarus buses, on which Moscow transport seems to rely, empires are like armies – the rank and file tends to march on its stomach.

But every Comecon country has its own special showcase in Moscow, its own department store which adds variety and a cosmopolitan thrill to the usual tedious round of Soviet shopping.

On a central street called Bolshaya Polyanka, which translates rather oddly as big little field, is the Polish store called Wanda and the Bulgarian one, Sofia. Wanda's reputation was built on Polish cosmetics – now less plentiful than they were – but this is still the place where Russian women buy their lip gloss and perfume and leather handbags.

The Bulgarians have two shops. Sofia sells mainly shoes and clothes, usually with better, brighter designs for summer than the Soviet stores can match. The other, Varna, seems popular mainly for its foods and wines. The Bulgarian Cabernet Sauvignon that sells for under £2 a bottle in Britain is snapped up here at almost twice the price. It retails under the name of Bear's Blood, a marketing trick borrowed from the Hungarian Bull's Blood.

One of the odder sights of these stores is to watch those dedicated shoppers, the Georgians and Armenians, shuffle round counter after counter in their carpet slippers. Moscow legend has it that their feet cannot stand the endless trek in ordinary shoes. They seem never short of money, and whenever the Yugoslav shop, Yadran, receives a shipment of particularly gross onyx and gilt table lamps, the Georgians make a concerted rush to pay over £300 a time.

Every shop has its speciality. The Hungarians are famed for their shampoos, skin creams, and baby oils. The Yugoslavs make the best and briefest bikinis. The Romanians sell good shoes, underwear and towels, and the East Germans sell the new status symbol, the food mixer.

The foreign stores are not restricted to Eastern Europe. India has two, selling saris and a vast range of incense which is becoming trendy among Moscow's young just as it was in the West in the 1960s. And for much the same reason – anasha, or hashish, is becoming more and more wide-spread and the incense helps mask the smell from the neighbours. So does the increasingly popular scent of patchouli, which also comes from the Indian shop on the river embankment opposite Kiev station.

You can buy Indian spices and curries at the shop attached to the Bombay restaurant, although the food cannot be recommended. The last meal I had there was a Chicken Kiev with weakly curried vegetables. But we are waiting for the redecoration of the Peking Hotel to end, when the restaurant is to re-open with Chinese cooks and ingredients.

Slowly, the Soviet authorities are starting to open this international shopping sector to new candidates. An American hamburger chain was planning to open a store here until the negotiations broke down at the last minute – not over Afghanistan or Poland, but over the Soviet insistence that they use Russian beef.

But Pierre Cardin has signed a contract to open a clothes store in Moscow, with goods priced in roubles for the well-heeled Soviet consumer.

The secret of this kind of commerce is to have a trade deficit with the Russians, against which the rouble earnings can be offset, so the Soviets do not have to fork out any precious hard currency to the foreigners.

Britain has a trade deficit with the Soviet Union now running at over £180 million a year. There is, after all, a Russian shop selling microscopes, radios and souvenirs in London's High Holborn. Since the guiding principle of Soviet diplomacy is reciprocity, a persuasive case could be made for opening a British store in Moscow.

My own selfish preference would be for a combined operation of Sainsbury's, Marks and Spencers, Oddbins, and W. H. Smith to offer their wares in Gorky Street. But, for obvious reasons, the Co-op might find it easier to plant the first British retail flag in Moscow.

When Mrs Thatcher told us all that in Mikhail Gorbachev she had found a Soviet politician with whom she could do business, she did not go on to specify the kind of trade she had in mind. But we are supposed to be a nation of shopkeepers.

Bazaar scenes
13 October 1986

We were serenaded by a military brass band as we went shopping the other day in one of the temporary village bazaars that have started to spring up in Moscow squares. We were unlucky – had we got there an hour earlier, we could have watched some acrobats and street theatre.

This was not one of the free markets where the peasants sell produce from their private plots at high prices. This was something new, a collection of gaily painted stalls, some designed in wig-wam shape, and some like the old Russian huts, selling fruit and vegetables at the controlled state prices.

This summer and autumn, there are few shortages. And because these new bazaars are made up of a number of stalls, there is no single long queue of the kind that makes the state shops so depressing.

Something rather dramatic has evidently happened to the distribution system. This summer, you could buy tomatoes in the state shops and in the new bazaars at 30 kopek (30p). In previous years, they were 50 kopeks – when you could find them – or you went and paid by the rouble at the free market.

Aubergines are down to 50 kopeks a kilo. You can find watermelons and plump grapes, and even the homely onions and garlic seem to have taken a quantum leap in quality.

As well as these fruit and veg bazaars, the state suppliers have started to sell fresh produce from the backs of lorries parked just outside the free markets and undercutting them in price. These trucks, with their number plates from Baku, Georgia, and the deep south, are coming directly from the collective farms to the Moscow consumer.

This is new, and so are the advertisements in the Moscow papers that say 'Attention housewives' and listing where the lorries will be, what they will sell, and at what price.

The takings at the free market have been falling sharply and the prices have started to come down too, except for items like parsley, radishes, and greens, and fresh pickles where the state system has not yet begun to compete.

I remember writing at the time of the Party Congress last March that we should see this summer whether the Gorbachev reforms to let the collective farmers sell their surplus produce were beginning to work. In Moscow, at least, the signs are more than promising.

But it took more than just this permission to make the system work. In Moscow, it took a series of measures by the energetic new party chieftain, Boris Yeltsyn. First, there was the massive corruption trial of most of the hierarchy of the city's trading department. Then he called in the new managers, harangued them about full warehouses while the shops were empty. And he told them to shift the goods or he would bring down the whole of the party committee to help them load the lorries.

Then he ordered the construction of these village bazaars, and insisted that they look attractive to the consumers. Hence the gay colours and the stages for street theatre. And he told them to challenge the stiff prices of the free markets by undercutting them at the market gates.

Now all of this may prove to be short-lived, and this winter we may get back to grim normal. And I have yet to learn whether this initiative is being repeated in other cities, but at least this year it has made Moscow a more pleasant place to live in.

But it has not stopped the grumbles. Another innovation is a series of new cooperative shops, known as the commercial stores, where high-quality foodstuffs can be bought for prices that are set midway between the subsidised state shops and the free markets.

What this means in effect is that the price of kolbasa, or

good meat sausage, has nearly doubled to 11 roubles. You cannot find real kolbasa in the state stores, only in the new commercial places.

And with constant rumours of sharp price rises in subsidised foods persuading people to buy as much as they can store, there are still shortages even of the rotten quality meat you find in the state shops at 2 roubles a kilo.

But in a Moscow still pleasantly surprised by seeing the state show a flair for retailing, the Gorbachev reforms are starting to pay off.

Head start
24 November 1986

My wife went shopping the other day and came back with four new hats. Nothing peculiar about that, you might say. Perhaps I should re-phrase it.

My wife went shopping the other day – an activity which most Western residents in Moscow reserve for the special foreign currency stores or the free markets where you can buy food from the farmers' private plots.

She happened to pass a new Russian shop called Moda, or fashion, selling Russian-made clothes for roubles to Russian women. This was not one of the token fashion workshops where diplomats' wives and very well-heeled Russians buy haute couture designs.

There are one or two of these privileged stores in Moscow, where the models swirl their clothes to disco music and copies of Italian *Vogue* lie casually on the table in the coffee house. They are not typical.

But my wife was shopping in a traditional working-class district of Moscow called Krasnaya Presnya. Since the days of the 1905 Revolution, when it was the fortress of the Moscow proletariat and was shelled to bits by Tsarist artillery for its pains, Krasnaya Presnya has taken pride in its working-class traditions.

So my wife went into this shop and looked at the fashions and liked what she saw and bought four of the mass-produced hats at reasonable prices. She paid less than 40 roubles (£42) for all four of them, which is about what we will be paying for two kilos of tomatoes come January.

And what is more, the hats were wrapped for her and then placed into two plastic bags of a tasteful purple and silver design that advertised the shop, its address, and phone number.

Even though she was then charged 60p for each bag, this is astonishing by Soviet standards. When we arrived here two years ago, plastic bags were virtually the equivalent of hard currency. Our London Airport duty-free bags, thrust at us with profligate abandon at Heathrow, were eagerly snapped up by Russian acquaintances.

I had hardly believed the account of a predecessor here, a *Times* correspondent, who wrote of sitting at the Moscow river beach and watching with disbelief Russian bathers swim out to retrieve and carry off a torn plastic bag in which the *Times* picnic had been wrapped. I have since observed the family of the concierge at our block of flats washing out the plastic bags in which we Westerners wrap our domestic rubbish before disposal.

Anyway, the designer plastic bag has come to the Soviet retail business, and jolly stylish they are too. But the hats were the real prize. I am no expert on hats for women, but I can report that there is a jaunty straight brim one that would look grand on a matador, and one that reminds me of photos of granny in the 1920s. I am assured that it is very fashionable.

Then there is the kind of pill-box number that Jackie Kennedy made all the rage when the American President was young and before the Beatles had been heard of. I think Bob Dylan wrote a song about it. And finally there is a creation with a hint of the Ku-Klux Klan about it that my wife refers to as the Spanish Inquisition hat.

What is more, they are starting to advertise this new Moda shop on the buses. For years, one of the distinctive features of Soviet life was the lack of adverts, but now you see ads for Pepsi-Cola and fashion shops on the sides of trams.

And on the Moscow City TV channel you can tune into the

advertising programme in the evenings, and read in the local papers about new shipments of Daghestan rugs and imported salami.

This is not to say that a consumer boom has started. It has been going for years, with almost every Soviet household having a TV set, and most having a refrigerator and a washing machine.

But the consumerism has assumed a new dimension. It is responding much faster to public demand, changing the styles and fashions of clothes much more frequently and offering much more choice.

Shortages and shoddy goods remain, however. Indeed, when my proud wife took some friends back to Moda to show off her new find, they found the same hats, but of much worse quality, with loose stitching and uneven brims, as if the machinery had slipped and not been reset.

But a new consumer demand is growing. As any husband will confirm, once a woman grows accustomed to buying stylish hats, a force is unleashed which the most determined politician would hardly dare to frustrate.

Bitter dregs
15 December 1986

There is a small cafe on Suvorov Boulevard, just along the tree-lined street from the Moscow Arts Theatre, where they do rather good macaroons. I called in the other day for some macaroons and a cup of coffee.

'No coffee, comrade. It's *defitzitny*.'

This is the universal Soviet word for a shortage of something. But then the girl said, 'We can offer you hot chocolate instead.'

Hot chocolate is normally so defizzitny I had never seen it before, so I took a cup and my macaroons, and paid over about 40p. Then I went to one of the chest-high tables to enjoy my snack, nodding at the gloomy Russian in a muskrat fur hat who stood stirring his chocolate.

'It's the planners' fault,' he said. 'They cancelled their orders of coffee from Brazil because they thought they would be able to get all the coffee we need from Nicaragua, and not have to pay out hard currency.'

I nodded. These days, Russians invariably refer to Nicaragua as 'nasha', or ours, like Cuba and Ethiopia and Vietnam and all the rest of the far-flung Soviet empire that costs them so much and profits them so little.

'But then Nicaragua has its own problem,' he went on. 'They wanted to sell their coffee for foreign currency too. And of course these days, they don't produce much coffee.'

Why not, I inquired.

'Socialism,' he said. 'It's a socialist country now, so there's less coffee. That's why I say: it's the planners' fault.'

The intermittent food shortages, and the queues that accompany them, are one of the great staples of Soviet conversation.

One of the great grumbles of this month is tea. Not the terrible Soviet tea from Georgia, which is still widely available, but the good Indian tea that the Russians love.

'We sent them Gorbachev – they could at least have let us have some tea in return,' goes one of the quips that you hear in the queues. 'He only went to Delhi to get a decent cup of tea – we know he doesn't drink vodka,' runs another.

My wife has started the great pre-Christmas bake-in, and went out for some butter. She fought to the head of the line to see the price, then queued at the cash desk to pay for two kilos worth, and then went back to the butter queue to hand over her receipt and get the stuff.

'No more than half a kilo per customer,' snapped the salesgirl, with that thoughtful courtesy so characteristic of the state service sector.

'Don't you worry dear,' said the other women in the queue. And as they came to be served their cheese or margarine, they each demanded their half kilo of butter and handed it straight to Julia.

In the vodka queues they are not always so kind, and indeed they can turn ugly, with windows being smashed and doors pushed in when the sales staff claim that stocks have run out. The shops usually have police outside these days, but it has not stopped the jokes.

'Remind me, what's the difference between an atom bomb and a neutron bomb,' says Igor.

'If they drop an atom bomb, then we won't be here and vodka won't be in the shop over there,' replies Oleg. 'But if they drop a neutron bomb, then we won't be here but the vodka will.'

'That's what I thought,' says Igor. 'So what sort of bomb has Gorbachev dropped that leaves us here, but no vodka?'

Then there is the one when Igor, after three hours queueing for vodka, explodes: 'That's it. I'm off to kill Gorbachev,' and he stomps off waving an old army revolver.

Three hours later he is back, looking downcast.

'Any luck?' Oleg asks him.

Igor shakes his head. 'No, the queue at the Kremlin to bump him off is even longer than the queue here.'

Delhi belly

20 July 1987

At last, we have a first-rate Indian restaurant in Moscow. We went along the week it opened, and had papadoms and fish tikka and dal and mango chutney and mutton curry and raita and hot nan, all washed down with Czech beer. We stuffed ourselves shamelessly.

There have been Indian restaurants in Moscow before, but like most of the token examples of international cuisine available in the Soviet capital, they have become very bad jokes indeed.

So, in the Bombay restaurant you were offered beef stroganoff or chicken kiev with lots of curry powder on top. In the Pekin restaurant, once the Sino–Soviet split saw the Chinese cooks go home, it was sweet and sour borscht, and in the Hanoi, we were once offered spring rolls that contained beetroot. Cabbage one can handle, beetroot is too much.

But the Delhi is different. It has just opened on the ground floor of a new building alongside a fashion showroom. It has the brightest and most attractive decor of any restaurant in the city, with Indian tiles and wall hangings and raga music and not a scrap of flock wallpaper or mock-mogul to be seen.

The Delhi is an early example of that fashionable new strategy in Soviet foreign trade, the joint venture. The Indian Tourist Board and the Moscow Restaurant Trust financed and now run the place as a partnership. The cooks and the waiters are Indian, as are the key ingredients of the food. The management and the cashiers are Russian, and thereby hangs the tale.

Soviet restaurants in general suffer from terribly slow service, and this is not entirely because of lazy waiters. There is a problem of organisation, because the Soviet tendency to overman every possible establishment puts a physical barrier between the waiter and the kitchen.

As you go into the kitchen of a Soviet restaurant, you will find a cash register, or at least an abacus, and a pair of scales and the kitchen cashier. The waiter does not simply collect the food from the cooks and take it direct to the customer. He takes it first to the kitchen cashier, who weighs the portions of food, and the waiter then pays for it, to be reimbursed by the customer when the bill is finally paid.

This lunatic system, which helps explain the lukewarm quality of most restaurant meals, has been slightly streamlined recently. The waiters now sign for each portion of food they pick up from the kitchen, but the kitchen cashier still has to weigh the grub and keep a separate set of books.

In big restaurants, you often see queues of waiters standing patiently before the kitchen cashier, and those of us who live in Moscow have grown accustomed to the system. We pass the time between courses by musing on the Russian sense of time, and telling laboured jokes about the dramatic pauses in Chekhov.

But the Soviet concept of kitchen book-keeping has come as a powerful shock to the Indian waiters of the Delhi restaurant, who have been trained in an entirely different tradition. The way the waiters smile and bow as a client enters, instantly flourish menus and stand attentively by the table, suggesting drinks, and being terribly eager to please is already the talk of Moscow.

For almost all Muscovites, such service is already more than enough. The subsequent delay between ordering the food and actually receiving it is accepted as part of the natural order of Soviet things.

It is then that the waiters come into their own. 'Most terribly sorry for the delays, sir. It is not us, and it is not the fault of the kitchens. It is the Russians,' we were assured in hushed voices. A long explanation of the kitchen cashier system then followed.

The food came, and it was delicious. The waiter then came by with three different kinds of chutney, offered more rice, more nan, and asked if anything else might tickle our palates. This sense of being waited upon by professionals who enjoyed their work and did it well was wonderful, but then we Moscow foodies are easily pleased.

When the plates were cleared away as soon as we had finished eating, there was the stunning realization that the waiter had kept an eye on the progress of our meal. Then he asked us if we had enjoyed the food, and seemed genuinely concerned that we should. He was followed by the Indian floor manager who made the same enquiry, explained further the problem of the delays induced by the kitchen cashiers, and told us of the Indo–Soviet managerial battles over the need to abolish the system. Most heartening of all was his calm assurance that the Indian concept of how to run a restaurant would inevitably prevail over the Soviet concept of how to run a bureaucracy and ensure full employment at the same time.

This is a culture shock for which Moscow may not yet be ready. And it will get worse this autumn, when the blossoming state of Sino–Soviet relations restores to the newly-rebuilt Restaurant Pekin the Chinese cooks and the weekly Chinese food deliveries via the trans-Siberian train.

Food fit for Tsars
10 August 1987

Whether in Britain or the Soviet Union, Richmond or Riga, I haunt second-hand bookshops looking for elderly volumes about old Russia.

One rattling good read that I found in a sleepy Lake District town is *The Dissolution of an Empire* by Meriel Buchanan, daughter of the British Ambassador at the time of the Revolution. Published in 1932, it was the first authoritative account of the way Lloyd George's government had rejected suggestions that the Tsar and his family be given exile in England, and it caused a great furore at the time. But the passage which caught my eye the other day was about the food prepared for the parties at the old Tsarist court.

'The zakuski were laid out on a long table, and taking a plate one would go from dish to dish, helping oneself, here to little mushrooms boiling in a rich cream sauce, here to one of the three different kinds of caviare, to cold smoked fish, to tiny salted cucumbers, small sausages served piping hot and flavoured with wine, cold vegetable salad, smoked salmon, ham prepared in some special way and stuffed eggs served with a delicious sauce,' she writes of a ball given by the Grand Duchess Marie Pavlovna in 1914.

Apart from the sausages flavoured with wine, which seems to have disappeared from the repertoire of the people's chefs, this could describe any modern Soviet 'koktyel'.

I have nibbled my way through more of these events than I care to remember. There have been parties at the state guest houses up on the Lenin Hills, with Moscow spread out below us, the Kremlin domes shadowed in the glare of the floodlights at the football stadiums. There have been smaller events at the Foreign Ministry, and at each of the main hotels, and I suspect that the chefs keep a copy of Miss Buchanan's book to hand to ensure that the traditional menu is maintained.

At the Praga Hotel at the end of the Arbat, there is a charming room known as the 'mirrored hall', where the grander foreigners tend to give their farewell parties, or at the

National, just across the Manezh Square from the Kremlin, most of the first floor is taken up with function rooms for these koktyel affairs.

Wherever Soviet catering stretches its palsied hand, the menu is recognizably the same as it was when the enchanting Miss Buchanan waltzed away the white nights of old St Petersburg.

There was a party at the National Hall just before the first night of the Royal Ballet tour here, and the tables groaned with red and black and grey caviare, with plates of salted cucumbers and sliced ham and endless smoked salmon, smoked sturgeon, and white and black bread. There were bowls of mayonnaise for the tiny shrimps and for the cylindrical portions of tinned crab.

The main change, of course, has been in the amounts of alcohol on offer. Miss Buchanan's account continued: 'All the time servants handed round small glasses of vodka, there was a buzz of conversation, a ripple of soft, subdued laughter, a sense of very delightful ease and enjoyment.'

These days, you will find aligned on the tables like so many toy soldiers, bottles of Soviet Pepsi-Cola, Russian lemonade, and the ubiquitous mineral waters from the Caucasus. If foreigners are organizing the event, then a few token bottles of vodka and Georgian white wine will probably be on hand.

Various Western travellers to the old Russian empire would always relate how they stuffed themselves on these zakuski, pronounced that they had dined exceedingly well, and were then much embarrassed when their Russian hosts led them to a second room for the real dinner.

It invariably began with soup, accompanied by sour cream and pastries, followed by fried sturgeon, followed by roast venison, and then by 'rabchik', the tree partridge, and a pudding of fruit and cream and nuts. I have never understood where the Russians, let alone their already stuffed foreign guests, ever managed to put this vast amount of grub. It leaves me with the same disbelieving admiration for the appetites of our ancestors that I get from reading Dickens on Mr Pickwick's banquets.

Miss Buchanan, too, used to find it was all too much, and she once complained to the French Ambassador of all the pomp and ceremony.

'Who knows how long it may last,' replied that wise gentleman. 'That Cossack standing behind the chair of the Grand Duchess – what a gorgeous bit of colour that scarlet soutane – he is a symbol of a vanishing tradition, and soon all that he stands for may be but a memory, and all this luxury and opulence which seems so secure and inviolate may vanish with him into obscurity.'

Well, it has and it hasn't.

Red hot

14 September 1987

I have written before about the Western goodies I bring in for Soviet friends. Now is the time to restore the balance and come clean about the Russian products I take out to friends back home.

Russian mustard is called 'gorchitsa' and it is the best I have ever tasted. It has the sharp bite of a good English mustard, the smoothness of French and, if this country could get its packaging and marketing acts together, it could do very well in the export trade. I always take a few pots back to the West and it has gained several fans.

Then there is 'khren', or Russian horseradish, which comes in a terrifying pink colour, with an almost explosive effect on the taste buds. It is an excellent condiment which I learned to appreciate through the considerate behaviour of waiters in Soviet restaurants.

They hate to rush their customers, and often allow you to build up a good appetite while sitting at table and waiting for an hour or so before they finally bring you the menu. To avoid starvation, I used to nibble bits of bread during this relaxing intermission from the cares of the day.

Then I began to experiment, putting bits of mustard on the bread and finally, in a spirit of exploration induced by an exceedingly long wait at the Tsentralny restaurant, I dipped some of my bread into the mysterious pink sauce. When my palate had bounced back from the ceiling, my sinuses had recovered and my eyeballs ceased whirling, I knew that an abiding love affair had begun.

Mr Gorbachev's thoughtful restrictions on the sale of alcohol have been widely misinterpreted in the West. I can now reveal that one of its central objectives was to introduce foreigners living in the Soviet Union to the delights of local mineral waters.

We had long ago come to an affectionate relationship with all the local vodkas. Not just the clear stuff that misguided Western barmen serve with tonic, orange juice and ginger ale, but the lemon-flavoured vodka, or my own favourite cold cure, the Pertsovka, steeped in red peppers. Then there is Old Vodka, and Hunter's Vodka, and indeed, a different vodka for every region in the country.

In a brilliant marketing strategy, which I commend to advertising executives throughout the West, Mr Gorbachev's new rules prevent us from having this stuff at lunchtime until the clock strikes 2 p.m. In the meantime, what is there to drink while nibbling our bread and mustard but the fizzy waters?

Forget your Perriers and your Highland Spas. The vast range of Soviet mineral waters are the finest in the world, My own favourite is Narzan, which comes from the foothills of the Caucasus mountains in the region of Stavropol, where Mikhail Gorbachev was born and raised.

Look no further for the secret of his success. He has been drinking the stuff for years, as you would expect from a man who made his career as First Secretary of a region which includes a large town which is named simply Mineral Waters.

It was Narzan that helped Gorbachev to the Kremlin. Yuri Andropov used to holiday in the mountain resort of Krasniy Kamni (red rocks) in Gorbachev's fief, taking the waters and feeling like a whole new KGB chief after the experience. Gorbachev would make his regular courtesy call on the visiting Politburo member, they would share a convivial glass of Narzan together, and the rest is history.

But there are many more brands to choose from. In Murmansk, I have had the local fizzy water, a thin and rather astringent drink as you might expect from the arctic regions.

Down in Azerbaijan, the fizzy water they call Badamli is so chock-full of minerals that you can never forget that the Caspian Sea contains salt water. The capital's own brand, Moskovskaya, is metallic enough to remind you of the place's industrial importance.

They all have a sovereign effect on the liver and the digestion and, after thirteen American diplomats here recently went down with a stomach bug from tap water diagnosed menacingly as 'a flagellate protozoon' known as Giardia, bottled water might be described as essential to one's health.

I read recently of some trendy chap in Los Angeles who had opened a non-alcoholic wine bar, which served mineral waters instead. The article did not relate whether he had discovered the inexhaustible potential of Soviet waters, but I offer the idea to any aspiring British entrepreneur, in exchange for a free glass of Narzan whenever my withdrawal symptoms become irresistible.

I would suggest they put on the bar little pots of Russian mustard and horseradish, and plates of good Russian black bread. And they might make use of the advertising slogan, Drink the stuff that put Gorbachev where he is today.'

Crusts with jam on

7 December 1987

One of the great mysteries of the Soviet life is the glaring contrast between the lack of food on sale in the state shops, and the lavish hospitality that you find in Soviet homes.

A major source for extra food is the free markets, where the cooperative farmers can sell their surplus crops at fancy prices. Meat (if you can find any) is currently 10 roubles a kilo at the market, compared to the state price of 2 roubles.

But there is another explanation – the zakazi, or reserve departments, of the major stores. I have written before of the way that large factories and ministries and institutes usually

have their own shop attached to their canteen, and the mor
the prestige or political blat, or influence, of the organization
the better the provisions on sale.

The zakazi departments are another arm of this system. Fo
example, all Soviets who work as drivers, secretaries an
translators for foreigners are assigned to us by an organizatio
called UPDK, and the UPDK trade union has zakazi rights a
nearby food stores. So UPDK workers in my office block ar
entitled to a monthly order of sausage, meat, sugar, jam an
butter and other hard-to-find or long-to-queue-for goods.

But the system has some curious ramifications. The bes
known food store in Moscow is Gastronom Number One o
Gorky Street, which everyone still calls Yeliseyev's, its pre
Revolutionary name when it was the Harrods of the city
Yeliseyev's does 70,000 individual zakazi each month. Th
major directorate of the Ministry of Interior gets 1200 each
week. The revision commission of the Finance Ministry get
100, and the State Committee on Trade Unions gets a weekl
600 orders. None of these organizations is based in th
borough of Frunzenaki which Yeliseyev's ought to be servicing

The organizations for war invalids, for heroes of the Sovie
Union, and the one for winners of the glory medal, each have
zakazi entitlement. And there is a new application on the stor
director's desk from one Petrov Sokolyanski, chairman of th
central book-lovers' society, asking for four senior officials o
his society to be given zakazi privileges at Yeliseyev's.

For these details, I am indebted to the new passion fo
investigative reporting among the staff of *Trud*, the newspape
of the Soviet trade unions. When the reporters arrived a
Yeliseyev's, the director demanded to see not only their pres
cards but also a formal letter from the paper authorising their in
quiry.

The nature of zakazi varies wildly. At times of state festivals
such as November 7, May Day or even New Year, vas
numbers of people are entitled to zakazi. War veterans alway
get zakazi, and single parents and invalids often do, and fo
many of them it is not a case of getting luxury or rare food, bu
of getting an assurance of basic supplies. For example, th
central locomotive depot is supposed to get 400 orders three
times a year. But this time the orders were refused becaus

they asked for tinned fish, mayonnaise and canned milk, which Yeliseyev's rightly argued was hardly prazdnichni, or festival food.

This is rather odd. First why are they ordering such basic foods, which are available at the state shops, and usually without too much queueing? Indeed, there was a recent press scandal about the millions of tons of canned fish that are still in the central depots, dating from the 1960s and still unsold. (The Ethiopians were sent a consignment as famine relief, but that is another story.)

The other question, naturally, is just which 400 workers at the huge central locomotive depot (which employs 1062 people) were given the right to zakazi at Yeliseyev's? As part of their investigation, the *Trud* reporters also went to Gastronom Number 26, where they reported that most of the zakazi customers were quite happy with the assortment of food products they could obtain, but the main complaint was the queueing.

'To buy your zakazi, one should queue in line outside for two to three hours, and then wait another hour on a long and narrow stair that leads to the cellar where they sell the food. This was the queue for war veterans,' *Trud* noted.

One can understand the sensitivity of the director of Yeliseyev's about all this. One of the great scandals of Leonid Brezhnev's *ancien régime* involved a former director of this food store, who became so rich from corruption that, for want of anything to spend the money on, he papered the walls of his flat with 100-rouble notes.

But the fear of official retribution seems to have faded somewhat. At least, the 580 employees of Yeliseyev's felt confident enough of their rights to have 700 zakazi assigned to themselves.

Vodka tonic

28 December 1987

Not being an abstemious sort of chap, I thought I knew my way around the labels on Soviet vodka bottles. There were the standard Stolichnaya and Moskovskaya export brands, the cheap domestic Rossiya vodka, and the flavoured red pepper and lemon varieties.

I had tried the light-brown starka, the strengthened vodka, and the hunter's vodka, and even the hard-to-find brands from the Ukraine. In Siberia, I had come across the rocket fuel they call 'spirit', and a chum who works on the Central Committee staff had even obtained for me a bottle of the exceedingly rare Admiralty brand.

But the bottle I was handed at a party recently, with a neatly-printed label that read 'granny's own', was a new one on me. The vodka had a slightly yellowish colour, it was highly-proofed and had a flavour that reminded me a little of sour-mash bourbon. A powerful and pleasant drink.

I looked at the label more closely, and saw that it listed none of the usual state factory provenance, and in fact it was rather more imaginatively designed than your usual Soviet product, with an etching of a smiling babushka seated beside a little wooden dacha, all very rustic and old Russia.

This was samogon, home-made moonshine, but tarted-up and marketed in a very professional, even entrepreneurial way, and this was something new. Ever since Gorbachev declared his new anti-alcohol campaign almost as soon as he became general secretary in 1985, they have been cutting the state production of vodka by about a third. And the home-distilling of samogon was the inevitable result.

So the first shortage in Soviet shops was sugar, and to this day, it is virtually impossible to buy loose sugar, rather than sugar cubes, which are less suitable for home distilling.

Then came the great yeast shortage, which has now become so serious that the leading women's magazine, *Rabotnitsa*, with a circulation of 17 million, has this month printed a recipe for making your own yeast to put in the special New Year cakes that Russian housewives are supposed to make at this time of year.

Apparently, the yeast shortage has made home baking almost impossible, so the recipe was a public service. But everybody has been talking of *Rabotnitsa*'s great service to the cause of samogon. Home distilling is a grand old Russian tradition, and the scale of this illegal production of moonshine boggles the mind.

Pravda recently ran an article that claimed that total national expenditure on alcohol was higher now than it had been before Gorbachev's clampdown. Certainly, some 4 million people have been arrested this year for drunkenness and the medical facilities to treat chronic alcoholism are being expanded under a new crash programme.

Even so, Gorbachev's crackdown has sharply reduced the numbers of drunks you see on the streets. In our first winter here, one of the great hazards of driving home at night, apart from the ice, was the way we had to weave the car around the log-like bodies of comatose drunks asleep in the road. Because there is no such thing as anti-freeze for windscreen wipers, in the good old days of plentiful supplies we used vodka, but added liquid detergent into the stuff to help deter the drunks who had learned that oblivion was to be found under the bonnets of foreigners' cars.

The sight of drunks was so commonplace in Moscow that I recall my daughter carefully explaining to a friend that the straps around tree-trunks had been placed there to give the drunks something to cling to as they crawled to their feet. In fact, they were meant to tie the saplings to stakes so they would grow straight, but Katie had seen so many drunks in the streets that the explanation seemed reasonable to her.

Oddly enough, Soviet alcoholics tend not to drink vodka, but the much cheaper fortified wines that say 'portwein' on the label, but which everybody calls 'barmatukha', or babbling-juice. Vodka now costs over ten roubles for a half-litre bottle, a steep price when the average wage is 50 roubles a week.

The price of the samogon home-brewed varies. A friend got me another bottle of 'granny's own' for 8 roubles, and I have heard of the stuff available for 5 roubles and less. But according to the little old ladies who usually get arrested for brewing the stuff, they make it not for money, but just to get by.

'I get a pension of 40 roubles a month, and I can't live on that, and the collective farm has stopped letting me have food or doing any repairs to my house, so what could I do?' said one little old lady who was interviewed on television after being busted by the police moonshine squad. 'I made some samogon and gave it to the farm shop manager and to the craftsmen and they let me have food and fixed the roof. They wouldn't do it for money, even if I had any, but samogon will get you by,' she chuckled.

10
Travel

Moscow is about as typical of the Soviet Union as New York is representative of the USA. Maybe less, because the Soviet Union is made up of fifteen different republics and over 100 official languages, and from one tip of the landmass on the Pacific Ocean to the other on the Baltic Sea the country stretches across eleven time zones. By train, it takes over a week to cross the Soviet Union.

Most of the time, I was stuck in Moscow, because that is where the news is made and released. And about one third of the country was closed to me and to all other foreigners for security reasons. This included a wide belt of land all around the frontiers (except at authorized crossing points), military training zones, the prison camp territories, and many big cities like Gorky, where Dr Andrei Sakharov was exiled or the industrial centres of Sverdlovsk and Chelyabinsk in the Urals. The real reason for closing these cities was that many of their factories were devoted to the defence industries. But they were also places where living standards and meat supplies were lower (according to Soviet friends) than in the cities on the tourist trail where Westerners were allowed to travel freely.

But I travelled wherever and whenever I could, going up to the arctic and down to the sub-tropics on the Caspian Sea and the Iranian border. I went out with the sable hunters about a thousand miles north of Lake Baikal in the heart of Siberia, and tasted the new wine vintages in the mountains of Georgia. I went to Kiev as they were still sluicing the streets and buildings against the Chernobyl fall-out, to the old mosques of the traditionally Muslim lands that Tamburlaine had ruled, and to the Russian Orthodox monasteries that had tried to defy Genghis Khan.

These Soviet provinces will eventually decide whether or n
Mikhail Gorbachev succeeds in his massively ambitious ar
risky attempt at a second revolution. The intellectual élite
Moscow may support his cultural thaw, and the journalis
and fashionable media people of the capital may praise h
reform plans, but the people out there in the closed cities ar
the endless steppes are the ones who will really decide.

A roll of the crumb on the scruffy steppe

22 September 1986

Until we drove through it, I had always assumed that th
steppes of the Ukraine would be rather like Noël Coward
Norfolk, very flat.

Well, parts of it are flattish, with those peculiar picturesqu
horizontals you get in France, or long avenues of tre
alongside the road and dotted copses and belts of trees a
windbreaks that impose interest on the view. But most of it
an endless rippling of soft swells, like a calm but powerful sea.

We drove from Odessa on the Black Sea coast up to the cit
of Kiev, and along the Dyesna river until we came opposit
Chernobyl, where the road forked to the east. It took us acros
the great battlefields around Kursk and Orel where the Re
Army had stopped the German Panzers in 1943, in what
still the biggest tank battle in history.

The steppe is lovely at harvest. You can see its rolls and fol
undulating into a blue distance, a little like the English down
But the roads here do not snake like Chesterton's 'rollin
English drunkard on the rolling English road', but hurt
forward, straight as a die. Straighter than the Romans bui
them.

The occasional village looks rather mean and dusty. Bu

they are not villages in our sense. There is no church or inn or little knot of shops to attract a traveller or to provide a focus for the community. There is usually a thin line of old women in headscarves sitting behind buckets full of tomatoes or apples or fat red potatoes.

The centre of road life is the petrol station, marked for a hundred yards in advance by the queues of trucks waiting to fill up. The drivers set up small barbecues to grill shashlik.

They're scruffy places, where you have to drive in first to see whether they have in stock any of the higher octane petrol for passenger cars. If you are lucky, you hand over your petrol coupons, and then serve yourself. The lavatories, like everywhere in the Russian countryside, are earth privies. A well-kept station is one that provides torn-up squares of *Pravda*. Usually, you have to bring your own.

This is a country where horses and carts are still common, jogging along the shoulders of the road, and where chickens peck their way into the middle of the road as you pass through the village to the vast fields where the combine harvesters roll like armies of tanks.

And some of these villages are lovely, tucked into a shallow valley, and nestling along the banks of a slow-moving river are the painted izbas, the old log cabins of the rural past with their carefully carved windows and stacks of firewood against the northern wall to dull the winter wind.

If this were the West, they would be country homes for wealthy cityfolk, or tea rooms or expensive restaurants offering nouvelle cuisine borscht. But in Russia you wait for the city outskirts to see the colonies of dachas, the country cottages that range from garden sheds in size to imposing two-storey wooden structures that look like Swiss chalets.

Apart from the farm machinery and petrol stations, the city's invasion of the steppe is impressed upon you in curious ways. You will suddenly come across a long line of school buses parked at the side of the road, and off in the distance are knots of schoolchildren doing their practical lessons in the economics of agriculture by picking potatoes.

As we drew nearer to Moscow, the traffic thickened, and we began to count the vast convoys of empty trucks, all with Moscow number plates, coming towards us. There were forty or fifty trucks in each batch, and in the 200 mile stretch from Orel to the capital we counted over forty of these convoys.

Like the schoolchildren and the army conscripts working in the fields, the trucks too had been summoned to help deal with the harvest. We followed them at a crawl, as loose potatoes and carrots and cabbages fell from the piled loads. At the radiation check points that have been installed since Chernobyl, the Geiger counter operators and the traffic cops could feed their families for a week on the vegetables that slid to the ground.

In the last petrol station, the *Pravda* in the privy carried a big editorial, headlined 'Everything ripe and grown – now to harvest and preserve it.'

Muslim in red

18 August 1986

Dunia Bekmuradova went out as evening fell to the courtyard of her home in the Turkmen village too small to have a name, poured petrol over her veiled head and struck the match. She finally died the next morning.

Perhaps she died for love, perhaps for a tribal and religious tradition far older than the Soviet state which has been trying to grapple with the implications of her death.

The village where she was born, grew to womanhood and died lies just on the Soviet side of the Afghan border, about 100 miles north of Herat. The women in this region still wear yashmaks, and although Dunia like most of her contemporaries paid her subscription to the Komsomol, the Young Communists' League, local custom proved stronger than ideology.

In this part of the Soviet Union, the traditional Muslim wedding feasts still take place and can still last for up to a week. But increasingly the feasts take a modern form which is known as a 'Komsomol wedding'. A Komsomol wedding means only that the guests sit on benches, rather than squat on the floor, and the bride in her pride of place daringly faces the guests.

Dunia's tragedy began when she was a schoolgirl and sent affectionate notes to a schoolmate, a bright young lad called Nur Mukhamed. Apart from telling her curtly that this was no way for a good Turkmen woman to behave, he ignored her. He went off to agricultural college, and while all of the other girls of Dunia's village were getting married and starting families, she was shunned.

She wrote to Nur Mukhamed, pleading with him to marry her 'if only for a year. Better to be divorced than to be what I am now, when nobody talks to me, and all believe that there was something between us.'

Nur Mukhamed came back to the village and was elected secretary of the Komsomol at the local collective farm. His relatives urged him to marry Dunia, since she was already disgraced for other men. His grandmother visited Dunia's parents to arrange the marriage.

But Nur Mukhamed refused and went off to the city to begin a promising career at party headquarters, in charge of a Komsomol section. Dunia and her mother followed, visiting the party secretary in their full regalia of yashmaks and robes to plead their cause. Still Nur Mukhamed refused, and so Dunia went home to commit suicide by fire.

It is a case that has thrown up all sorts of questions about the relationship of Muslim tradition to the Soviet state, about the success of modern education in raising a new, secular generation of Muslim youth. And, more immediately, it has brought into the public gaze the sheer power of custom in the Soviet Union's own deep south.

Komsomolskaya Pravda has devoted a long article to the officially illegal practice of kalym, or a dowry for the bride. Local officials in Turkmenia acknowledged that they could not think of a wedding where kalym had not been paid.

'A sum of 20,000 roubles (nearly £20,000) is considered quite modest, allowing matters to be arranged more or less decently,' the paper noted. 'And these days, kalym is not money alone. On the eve of marriage, the families make up agreed lists which include items such as gold teeth for the bride, a 'profitable' job for her elder brother, or fixing the admission to an institute for her young brother.'

With mounting disbelief, *Komsomolskaya Pravda*'s reporter began questioning local party officials, and found some of them making a staunch defence of the practice.

'Young families founded on such arrangements made by their parents are much stronger, thanks to kalym, than marriages for love. The kalym money is spent on buttressing the material comforts of the newly-weds, allowing them to set up a proper home. Since this strengthens the family, such customs are progressive,' one local party official is quoted as saying.

Brides, apparently, feel undervalued and even disgraced unless their kalym is high. And in the case of poor Dunia, the disgrace was all the greater. Her reluctant swain, Nur Mukhamed, has seen his career fall into ruin.

He is now serving a four-year prison term passed by a local court, for reasons which remain as obscure, but doubtless as powerful, as the mysterious old traditions of Soviet central Asia.

Tallin tales
29 September 1986

The party was meant to bring together the bolder spirits of the new wave among the artists of the Soviet Baltic republics. But almost as soon as they arrived, the contingents from Latvia and Lithuania made a bee-line for the back room where the TV was showing the credits for the latest episode of *Dynasty*.

It was a long night. After *Dynasty* came the *Benny Hill Show*, and then *Miami Vice*. And before the late night rock video programme began, there was the news in Finnish. Being accustomed to Finnish TV, the Estonians just go on with the party.

Helsinki lies less than fifty miles to the north, and Finnish TV beams across the choppy strait into the homes of the 1.5 million Estonians who all seem much more at home in Finnish or English than they are in Russian.

The ferries that bring the weekend Finns to the Estonian capital of Tallin also bring the jeans and designer track-suits, the jogging shoes, tights and cosmetics that make this ancient trading port – one of the Hanseatic League cities that dominated medieval commerce – the best-dressed city of the contemporary Soviet Union.

It remains a surprise in a Soviet city to be woken up by church bells on a Sunday morning, to stroll through an old town that has been lovingly restored, to smell roasting coffee and fresh baking in the streets, or to pop into a tiny bar inside the city walls for a glass of hot mulled wine.

We Westerners who live in the Soviet Union tend to notice only when we get back to the West how certain of our senses have atrophied. We have lost the knack of living in the consumer society, and get stunned by the lights and sounds and blare of advertising even at London airport. We shop compulsively, yet get confused by the vast range of choice, yearn for decent restaurants, but dither helplessly over menus.

The only place in the Soviet Union where we start feeling these strange symptoms is in Tallin, where the cafes are stuffed with fresh cream cakes, and the food shops offer a range of salamis that are only available in Moscow for hard currency, and not always then. Tallin even boasts a new unisex fashion store called Mood, offering unheard-of things like white three-piece suits for men and stylish clothes for women with hugely padded shoulders.

And like its neighbour on the Baltic coast, the Latvian capital of Riga, Tallin not only boasts the medieval old town, but also what can only be described as an upper-class suburb of large detached homes set in parkland. The area is inhabited, overwhelmingly, by Estonians, while the Russian immigrants tend to congregate in the ugly new high-rise districts.

On Sunday afternoon, the leafy suburb of Nomme was having its sports day. Horses trotted around for the gymkhana, there was a welly-throwing competition and kids' races, and the truck selling take-away shish-kebabs and dumpling stew was doing good business. Some idiots had thrown an old tyre on to the bonfire and thick black smoke drifted across the field to the stage where the local punk rock group, Big Sister, was thumping out an outrageous version of 'Get it on'.

I strolled round the field with an Estonian friend who talked gloomily about the future prospects for Estonian prosperity. His parents made their money mainly from their greenhouses, where they grow flowers for private sale. Their current house, with its private sauna in the basement, its Western TV and video, and its collection of antique clocks and eighteenth century china, had all come from flowers.

His own lifestyle, which included a new Lada hatch-back, designer clothes and a video camera, was funded by his moonlight work as a disco entrepreneur. Officially, his pay for presenting a disco night was 98 kopeks (just under £1). In fact, everybody knew that a decent disco cost at least 50 roubles in cash. And, since he offered a video disco, with a big-screen TV and the latest video clips recorded from Finnish TV, he could make 150 roubles a night.

But the growing crackdown on what the Kremlin calls unearned incomes, and the new checks on just where the money was obtained before you can buy a new house, or build a new dacha, or buy another antique clock, was putting a cramp in everybody's lifestyle.

A neighbour of his who had just bought one of the pleasant suburban houses for 70,000 roubles (£70,000) had already faced a rather tricky interview over his earnings. The man worked at the local car-servicing centre, which is widely known as a licence to print money from its access to spare parts and private servicing.

Hitherto, the socio-political consequences of Soviet citizens freely watching capitalist TV have been blunted by Estonia's relative prosperity. But it may not last.

Autumn of the patriarch
6 October 1986

As you come over the brow of the last hill and see the monastery-city of Zagorsk sprawling arrogantly ahead, you start to understand what the Mongols felt. And all the other invaders. The Poles and Lithuanians besieged the place for sixteen months nearly four centuries ago. And they never broke in to loot this treasure house of Russian culture.

With the golden domes glinting in the sun, the place reeks of wealth and the precious offerings that accumulated from generations of piety. Its vast fortress walls, over 30 feet high and studded with watchtowers and slits for the archers, are clearly protecting something of enormous value.

Forty miles north-east of Moscow, Zagorsk is the fortress of the old Orthodox Church militant. Founded over six centuries ago by St Sergei, it became the linchpin of the chain of monastery-fortresses which ringed Moscow and made up the city's defence against the Tartars.

It has been a key to Russian history ever since. When Moscow and its Kremlin fell to the Polish invaders, Zagorsk held out and became the base for the national uprising that threw them out again.

Boris Godunov is buried here, and the young Peter the Great made it the residential headquarters of his own struggle for power. Its walls contain three cathedrals, smaller churches, a Tsar's palace, a hospital and a monastery, and to this day it is the centre of the Orthodox Church, the residence of the patriarch, the main seminary and theological academy.

It is also a strange kind of refuge for the mad and crippled and those transported by religious fervour. Last week, we saw two old women wrestling each other to the ground before the shrine in the cathedral of the Dormition. They were arguing over precedence – which was to kiss the floor first.

On earlier visits, I had seen drunks retching in the yard by Boris Godunov's grave, and mentally deficient children being urged up the cathedral steps on their knees by their devout grandmothers. I have not yet been to Zagorsk without some intervention of the grotesque, some scene which harks back to the medieval, a reminder of the visceral force of old Russia in the midst of the Soviet state.

Zagorsk is about to lose a part of that precedence which gives it magic. In time for the 1000th anniversary of the founding of Christianity in Russia, in 1988, the residence of the patriarch and the administrative centre of the Orthodox Church are to be moved from Zagorsk to the newly-restored Danilovsky monastery in central Moscow.

It was probably inevitable that the superstitious should have begun the rumour of divine displeasure at Zagorsk's imminent demotion to account for the mysterious fire which broke out in the monastery last weekend, and which killed five young seminarians. It began in the early hours of the morning, in the seminary, and the official version is that swift and skilful action by the fire brigade prevented any major damage to the buildings and art treasures. The seminary lectures were able to begin on schedule on Monday morning.

Tragic as the news is, we should all be grateful that the cathedrals and museums are undamaged. Even more than the Moscow Kremlin, the Trinity and St Sergius Lavra monastery (to give it its pre-Revolutionary name) embodies the culture of Russia. You can stand in one spot and see the development of Russian architecture, from the Holy Trinity cathedral of the 1420s, to Ivan the Terrible's Dormition cathedral of the late sixteenth century.

The great icon painter Andrei Rublev painted his master-pieces here, and the museums of the monastery are an enchantment in themselves, ancient embroidery giving way to icons, to centuries of the local woodcarvers' art. The place is an instant and total immersion in everything that made the Russians what they were, and what they remain beneath the Soviet veneer.

It is a reminder of how very different they are from the rest of the Europeans. Their religion came from Byzantium and the East, and not from Rome and Luther. They missed the great cultural storm of the Renaissance, and only belatedly began to join the European cultural mainstream with the Enlightenment.

But in the end, you remember the solid stone walls of Zagorsk – the role of church as defender. Had it not been for the sturdy monasteries of old Russia, our ancestors in the West might never have had a Renaissance or a Reformation. Just as the modern Soviet state is filled with reminders of the price they paid to stop Hitler, Zagorsk reminds us of the older, enormous price they paid for saving medieval Europe from the Mongols.

The desperate pain in the heart of Russia

29 December 1986

The cruellest Soviet joke I ever heard was told to me by a Russian as we strolled around the streets of Tallin, capital of the Baltic republic of Estonia. Like so many Soviet jokes, it begins with Reagan and Gorbachev sitting and chatting by a summit fireside.

'In the USA, we have one private car for every three people,' says Reagan.

'So what,' replies Gorbachev, 'in Estonia, we too have one private car for every three people.'

'In the USA, one family in three owns its own second home in the country,' says Reagan.

'So what,' replies Gorbachev, 'in Lithuania, too, every third family owns a second home in the country.'

'In the USA, five people out of every hundred are dollar millionaires,' Reagan perseveres.

'So what,' replies Gorbachev, 'in Georgia, five people in every hundred are rouble millionaires.'

'What is this?' Reagan interrupts. 'I keep talking about the whole USA and you just talk about Estonia and Lithuania and Georgia. What about the Russians?'

'How dare you!' snaps Gorbachev. 'Have I asked you about how the blacks live in America?'

This joke is too true to be funny. The Soviet Union is a bizarre kind of empire, where the colonized, whether Eastern Europeans, the Baltic people or the trans-caucasians of Georgia and Armenia, enjoy a very much higher standard of living than the Russian imperialists back home.

This does not apply to the privileged cities of Moscow and Leningrad, but they are barely pimples on the vast face of the Russian Republic. By far the biggest of the fifteen separate republics that make up the USSR, Russia stretches from the Black and Baltic Seas to the Pacific, and takes in whole sub-continents along the way.

And it has its problems. This summer, Mikhail Gorbachev made a rapid tour of the Soviet far east, and slammed into the local party chiefs for making the local workers wait ten to fifteen years for a flat, for not providing schools and hospitals and public services, and for provoking a steady emigration from the very region which needs a big and growing population if its wealth is ever to be exploited.

In the heavy industrial belt of the Urals, the cities of Sverdlovsk and Chelyabinsk and the surrounding iron and steel regions make up the Soviet black country. These cities began to explode under Stalin's industrialization plans in the 1930s, grew even faster under the strain of war, when they were remote from Hitler's bombers, and have provided the country's metallic muscle ever since.

As a result, in spite of a handful of advanced machine tool workshops and relatively high-tech defence industry plants, this smokestack region is already promising to be the rustbelt of the 1990s. It will have to go through the strains of massive retraining of an obsolescent workforce and reinvestment in modern machinery just at the time when its own ore resources are running thin, and being replaced from the new supermines that are being developed in Eastern Siberia.

The social strains in these smokestack cities are already apparent. One of the many odd features of Soviet society is that its highest crime rates are not recorded in the biggest cities, which is the case in most other countries in the world, but in the cities of medium size. There are some explanations for this – such as large numbers of police in Moscow and Leningrad, and their lion's share of theatres and cinemas and social amenities compared to the regional cities.

The capital cities of the smaller republics do much better in this regard, because local republican pride insists that each maintain a republican ballet company, an opera house and a theatrical centre of its own. Sverdlovsk has opera and Perm has ballet. But pity then the Ufas and Gorkys and Chelyabinsks which have the population, but lack the social pastimes and pleasures to keep them occupied.

The evidence for the social problems of the Urals black country is anecdotal, partly because of the difficulty of collecting comparative statistics, and because so much of this area is closed to foreigners. But from the Soviet press, and from the tales of Soviet friends who know the area, one can build up a picture of a region that seems grimly similar to the depressed industrial northern cities of Britain.

They seem to share everything except the unemployment. But the drug abuse, the teenage vandalism, the broken marriages and depressing lack of amenities, the poor public housing and the general sense of despondency make them brothers under the grimy industrial skin.

A friend of mine, a young musician who has made the occasional tour of this black country, calls them 'the desperate cities'. And some young Russian journalists I know who are currently compiling *Komsomolskaya Pravda*'s latest readers' poll of the year's favourite pop songs, gave me another insight. 'The mail always comes overwhelmingly from these smaller industrial cities, and they always tip the balance towards the established big-name stars like Leontiev and Pugacheva,' one said. 'But the readers were nominating songs we had never heard of. New songs, but they weren't on record or cassette. We checked, and found these were songs that had been sung once on TV in the last two or three weeks. The TV is all the kids have out there. The shops are short of records, there are few discos or concerts. It's a TV culture. It is more than just TV. It is from Chelyabinsk that a curious rock group calling itself 'Bad Boys' (in English) export their underground tapes, with their lyrics that run 'kill all the commies and the Komsomol too'.

These are the cities from which come bizarre letters to the Moscow papers, from defiant young gangs who call themselves Nazis, confident that in the Soviet state this is the ultimate obscenity with which to shock their elders. (But then I have sat in a Moscow cinema to watch *Battle of Moscow* and heard the teenagers cheer every time Hitler appeared on screen.)

There are more clues to the social strains in the Soviet black country from the policy of glasnost in the official press. We read more about violent crime, about the armed bank raid in the city of Perm that killed a policeman, of the attempted aircraft hijacking in Ufa in which two drug addicts shot dead two police sergeants and killed two passengers before being shot themselves. We learn more of the scale of the drug problem, or of the growing numbers of orphans abandoned by single mothers, of teenage vagabonds and female alcoholism.

It is tempting to see all this as a geographical strain between the cold north against the fertile and sunny south, the same kind of shift of prosperity towards the sun which has happened in Western Europe and in North America. But in the Soviet Union, the process is complicated by the prosperity of the northern republics of the Baltic, of Lithuania and Estonia, who sneer at their Russian immigrants as *gastarbeiter* who have come in to do the menial jobs of construction and public services.

Russia explains the prosperity of other republics in a variety of ways. The Baltic peoples, they say, have been part of Europe for centuries, and have traditions of trade and manufacturing and a Germanic sense of social cohesion which makes them more efficient. The Georgians and Armenians have the good climate to produce fair crops and a commercial tradition that makes them rich. Even the Muslim republics have the solidarity of extended families and the cohesion of Islam.

It is ironic that this growing disparity between Russia and its provinces is becoming apparent just at a time when the Russians are about to lose their traditional majority status among the peoples of the Soviet Union. It remains, thanks to the Ukrainians and Belorussians, an overwhelmingly slavic country for the moment, although the high birth rates of the Muslim lands threatens to change that.

And at the same time, the Russians as a people are faced with the challenge of the new phase of industrialization that Mikhail Gorbachev has promised. The heart of Soviet industry lies in European Russia and the Urals, and we all know the social strains that Western Europe has undergone in these last ten years of industrial re-organization.

Gorbachev is determined to whip the country into the post-industrial age by the year 2000. The problem is that, more than any other part of the country, the Russians have not yet absorbed the social tensions that came with the first crash programme of industrialization. Rightly famous for their endurance, the punchdrunk Russian people have a whole new challenge to face.

High spirits
12 January 1987

My wife was worried. I had got home late from the office partly because it was so cold it took a long time to start the car, and also because the drive home was treacherous and slow.

'The hot water has been off for three hours, and now the heating pipes are cold,' she said. The flat was cooling fast. I kept my coat on as I checked with neighbours that their heating had also gone off. I rang the Russian caretaker, who said that the emergency services were working on it.

What about our children? Keep them in bed, well wrapped up, and put their fur hats on, was his advice.

Outside, it had just hit minus 40°C. That is very cold indeed. In our all-electric flat we could not even turn the gas taps on ... I remembered what Russian friends had said about the last big freeze when whole blocks of flats were evacuated.

But then there was a groaning in the pipes and the warmth began to return. I felt like cheering.

Normally, I relish the approach of a Moscow winter. I have taken up cross-country skiing since arriving here, and have learned to love the Russian landscape under snow, the astonishing radiance of the winter sun filtered through the bare birch trees, the taste of cold vodka after a long run, the sweet pain of warming myself at a picnic fire deep in the forest.

This year it has not been like that. We had our first snow in September, which lasted for two days and then gave way to an Indian summer. In November and December, we had snowfalls that melted in sudden thaws. It was wet and cold and nasty.

The babushkas, the all-powerful and all-knowing Russian grannies who really run the country, began to prophesy last summer that this winter would be the coldest and most fearsome for years.

The squirrels began collecting their nuts early, and in unheard-of quantities, they said. The red berries in the forests were two and three times more plentiful than usual, an infallible sign that Mother Nature was preparing winter food stocks for the poor birds.

Certain kinds of mushrooms were thick on the ground this autumn, they said, and I forgot what it was the pine cones were said to be doing, but this was another reliable sign that this winter was going to be a real stinker.

Forty degrees Centigrade below, the babushkas cackled, and then they poked me hard in the chest and said, 'Don't let me see you or your children going around without a good fur hat, young man.'

Forty degrees below freezing. I last came across that kind of temperature when I was in central Siberia, about a thousand miles north of Lake Baikal. And there I heard that mystical, marvellous sound that the Russians call the 'whisper of stars'. It is the rustling and crackling noise your breath makes as you exhale, and the water vapour instantly freezes into ice crystals and falls tinkling to the ground.

Siberians are quite mad when it comes to winter. Having listened to the whispering of the stars I was quite ready to get back into the jeep and cower around the heater. My host insisted on an open-air picnic.

I was put in charge of the Spirit, a Siberian super-vodka that is as near pure alcohol as makes no difference. In my view, Spirit explains the success of the Soviet space programme – rocket fuel cannot compete.

I nursed the Spirit, while my hosts built a fire, piled snow into the cauldron, and began to whittle flakes of deep-frozen fish into what became a delicious stew. Some salt, some potatoes and dried herbs, a few slugs of Spirit and we became a very merry party.

Then it came time to take a pee. I trudged through the snow to a discreet distance, and began a long process of unbuttoning several layers of garments. Finally, all was ready. And I watched in disbelief as a thin but sturdy stalagmite of quick-frozen urine began to ascend towards me.

At moments like this, your entire past life tends to flash before you – or at least those bits where knowledgeable people told you about frostbite, what it did to the affected part, and whether the damage was reversible. At this point memory failed me and panic ensued.

I began to flounder slowly backwards, away from this growing pillar of ice. It followed me with obvious menace. I retreated further, stumbled, tripped and fell, just as Siberia's rival to the Leaning Tower of Pisa collapsed on to the snow and lay there in the shape of a large question mark.

Understandably shaken by this experience, I hurried back to the campfire, where my friends had become so hysterical with laughter that one of them fell over and knocked down the last bottle of Spirit, which was probably just as well.

Georgia on my mind
30 March 1987

In the unlikely event of being asked, I would have to turn down any request to act as Mrs Thatcher's guide around Georgia, one of my favourite parts of the world, let alone the Soviet Union. She will be spending some eight hours in the capital of Tbilisi, which will be delightful enough, but she is missing the best of the place.

She ought to begin with what was the old Georgian capital of Mxheta, until the upstarts from Tbilisi assumed that role in the fifth century AD. But the hilltop Cathedral of the Cross at Mxheta, which dates back to the late sixth century, is one of the world's most impressive sights, rising squatly from a barren peak. It symbolises the embattled history of lonely Christian Georgia, always fated to stand at the point where the great empires of Turkey, Persia and Russia met and disputed.

Tbilisi itself was plundered twenty-nine times in its history by various invaders. The armies of Genghis Khan and Tamburlaine the Great both passed this way, and after a tangled history the place was ruled by the Persians until the eighteenth century, when the Russians took over, at the invitation of the Georgian royal family.

In Mxheta, having seen the chapel in the cathedral where the robe of Christ is said to lie and the handprint in stone of the tenth-century master mason, Arsukidze, who calls himself 'Slave of God', we could lunch at the best restaurant in the Soviet Union.

The Marani was one of the first of the experimental new co-op restaurants, which means it is very nearly private. The staff pay 40 per cent of their profits in rent and taxes and keep the rest. They have their own small farm to produce fresh fruit and vegetables, eggs and chickens. They make their own wine, and buy in the better vintages like Stalin's two favourite sweetish, heavy reds, Kinzma-Aruli and Hvanchkara. They buy their fresh meat and fish in the market, share out the profits and do rather well for themselves.

The place is designed along the lines of the traditional semi-subterranean homes with a dome-shaped roof, often covered in turf, which presented a useful low profile in a country that was comprehensively invaded so often. Inside, there is pleasant rustic furniture, an open fire made fragrant with vine twigs and apple wood, and excellent, attentive service.

We should then drive on another sixty miles to Gori, the birthplace of Stalin, and the last place in the Soviet Union where you can still stand in the shadow of one of the vast statues to the old dictator which used to pepper the country. The humble house of his birth is now surrounded protectively by a miniature marble Parthenon.

Behind it stands the Stalin Museum, which gives an understandably one-sided portrait of his life as brilliant seminary student, poet, young revolutionary, political prisoner under Tsarism, Lenin's right hand, father of his people and great war leader. One of the most surreal sights in the entire country is the final room in the museum. A shrine to the man, it is almost pitch dark, lined in deep purple velvet.

At first you see only a painting of Stalin on his death bed, and then as you grope forward, a great pit opens to the right, again lined with velvet. It contains only a slim white plinth with a gleaming brass death mask gazing serenely upon the semi-circle of white marble pillars which ring the pit like so many prison bars. At the centre, the pillars are broken off, allowing the visitor to peer in, and muse on the uncanny feeling that this is a broken cage from which some fearsome beast has escaped.

It will be impossible for Mrs Thatcher to avoid the lingering presence of Joseph Stalin, even in her eight hours in the city. But there is one room in the museum, containing marvellously wrought gold jewellery, which I would commend to her as a reminder that there have been other illustrious visitors to these parts. The gold dates from the age of myth, when that part of Georgia that adjoins the Black Sea was known as the fabulous and rich land of Conchis, whence Jason and his Argonauts obtained their golden fleece. The three decades of Stalin, seventy years of Soviet power, and the two centuries of Russian suzerainty, are all but a fleeting moment in the history of ancient Georgia.

The lessons of Chernobyl: the tomb which Russia rues

22 April 1987

Just outside Moscow, at the Mitinskoye cemetery, there is a row of twenty-six white marble headstones. They stand above the graves of people who died from the most intense blast of nuclear radiation ever suffered by human beings in peace time.

Six of the headstones carry a gold star, to mark the graves of the firemen who died fighting the blaze that followed the world's worst nuclear accident. The oldest was twenty-eight.

At Chernobyl now, the vast concrete tomb that surrounds the stricken reactor stands like some ghastly war memorial over a nuclear park that still bustles with activity. A stone's throw away, men are still working, trying to decontaminate and prepare the neighbouring reactor to go back into service later this year.

A few hundred yards across the flat plain, two more reactors of the same design have been back on line for months, pumping electricity into a Soviet power grid that is always hungry for more. A little further away, the construction teams are already working on the foundations of two more nuclear power stations that will make the Chernobyl nuclear park into one of the biggest sources of energy on the Euro–Asian land mass.

The Soviet Union has little choice but to persevere with nuclear power, in spite of the terrible warning it received at Chernobyl last April. The country's raw materials and energy resources lie in the far east and north. Its factories arc concentrated in the west, and the fastest growing part of the population is in the south. To get the raw energy to the people and factories that need it imposes a monstrous cost. The Chernobyl nuclear park was the logical answer, putting the power source close to its market.

But the accident barely a hundred miles north of Kiev, the third biggest city in the country, put millions of people at risk. Indeed, the risk has only just subsided. This week, Izvestia reported that the peak of the spring floods had passed without sluicing radioactive silt into the main waterway of the river Dnieper.

The raw cost of the Chernobyl disaster has been put by the Soviet authorities at thirty-one lives, and over 2000 million roubles (about £2 billion). But there are other costs to be paid.

The trials have already been announced for the nuclear technicians who are being blamed for the disaster. The other RBMK reactors like Chernobyl with their graphite-moderated systems have been consecutively shut down as new safety and control systems are installed. Across the country, the scientists and technical staff who run the Soviet nuclear power stations have been going through special safety courses in an attempt to ensure that the human error being blamed for the disaster should never happen again.

There was a palpable sense of relief in Vienna last August at the grand post-mortem on Chernobyl conducted by the international nuclear power industry at the conference of the IAEA, the International Atomic Energy Association. Western and Soviet nuclear power specialists must have feared that their careers and their whole industry were at risk. The official finding, that the technicians of Chernobyl had 'engaged in unauthorised experiments', amounted to a reprieve for the principle of nuclear power.

That conference also amounted to a reprieve for the image of Mr Gorbachev's reform programme in the Soviet Union. His promise of glasnost looked like a sick joke in the three days of silence that followed the Chernobyl disaster.

The accident took place just after 1 a.m. on the Saturday morning. The first public alarm bells began to ring on the Monday, when Sweden announced the dramatic surge in radiation levels. Not until the Monday evening, in spite of urgent government-to-government appeals from the Swedes, and formal inquiries from the IAEA in Vienna, did the Soviets admit, in a terse two-sentence statement on the television news, that there had been an accident.

Official Moscow certainly knew of the disaster within hours. Academician Valery Legasov, deputy director of the Institute of Atomic Energy, was despatched to the scene on the first Saturday, along with the deputy minister of the interior for the Ukraine, General Genbady Berdov, and Air Force General Nikolai Antoshchkin. He was told to prepare a massive fleet of helicopters to stand by to help seal off the spewing reactor by 'bombing' it with sand and mud and lead pellets.

Moscow's three days of silence, as the radiation began to drift across northern and western Europe in a foul and invisible cloud, stands as a monstrous indictment of the Soviet system. The lack of information made available to their own people, in spite of the understandable fears of a mass panic, was simply shameful. I shall never forget going down to the Kiev railway terminal in Moscow and seeing train after train arrive, each one crammed with children, as the parents of Kiev arranged the evacuation that Soviet officialdom was delaying.

But as the days of May went by, and it became clear that the armies of scientists and experts and soldiers were slowly bringing the rogue reactor under control, the world's renewed condemnation of the Soviet system began slowly to give way to a reluctant admiration.

There was the plain courage of the firemen who stayed on to fight the flames as their radiation counters went off the clock. There was the skill of the scientists who managed to face and solve technical problems that had never been posed before as they battled against the nightmare of a meltdown. And slowly, the Soviet press and television began to show that glasnost did have meaning, as brave TV cameramen and some tenacious news reporters from *Izvestia* gave the Soviet people and the rest of the world some sense of the horror and the heroism.

As the Soviet system began to cope with the disaster, I had a sudden sense that a familiar process was under way, that something was being re-enacted that I had read about. It was the old Russian steamroller in a new guise, a lumbering and secretive and insensitive system reeling back in shock and disorganization, but then with slow and awesome strength beginning to gather and mobilize its immense reserves and to fight back.

But that same centralized system of government and authority which organized the Soviet steamroller into withstanding and overcoming the threat of Chernobyl has also decided, without any consultation, that the country's need for nuclear energy means that the people must live with the constant menace of an expanding nuclear power programme. If Mr Gorbachev's tentative experiments with democracy are to continue, it could be interesting to see what the Soviet public thinks.

As Chernobyl revealed the limits to glasnost, it is likely also to emphasise the limits on democratization. But then, who ever suggested a British referendum on building Sizewell B, or asking the American voters whether to rebuild Three Mile Island. Nuclear power and democracy are not easy bedfellows. And that, too, is a part of the Chernobyl legacy.

The fear of war brings good times to Murmansk

29 October 1985

The arctic city of Murmansk is the neon-light capital of the Soviet Union, the blues, greens and reds flashing in the drab northern darkness. They advertise Aeroflot and the Arctic Shipping Line and proclaim the victories of Leninism. They cast lurid glows over the vegetable stalls where fresh lemons are plentiful, at almost 80p each, although Moscow has been without them for weeks.

There are fresh tomatoes and cucumbers on the stalls, some of them grown in the huge greenhouses of the local state farm, where they tell you proudly that they get a better yield per acre than anywhere else in the Soviet Union. The people of Murmansk can afford the prices, with their bonuses for living in this arctic city which sees no daylight for ten weeks each winter.

Salaries are generally twice as high as in Moscow. The greenhouse farm manager earns 800 roubles a month. 'As much as a minister,' he says shyly. Merchant and fishing fleet officers earn a minimum of 600 roubles a month (about £600), and more than three times the country's average industrial wage.

Seamen on the arctic route can take home 1000 roubles a month, so Murmansk is one of the richest cities in the Soviet Union. Its department stores are crammed with refrigerators, crystal glasses, and expensive rugs from Vietnam and Kazakhstan.

But the main goods on show in the Univermag shop window on Lenin Avenue are naval shirts and peajackets and smart mariners' hats. The streets are filled with black-uniformed naval officers. Although the port of Murmansk contains only merchant vessels and the vast fishing fleet, just up the long thin fjord that leads to the open sea is the headquarters of the Northern Fleet at Polyarny. The main business of the 420,000 people who earn high wages to live way up here near the 70th parallel is to support the Soviet Union's biggest naval base.

Murmansk has been a child of war from its very beginning, just seventy years ago, when the Tsarist government was being battered by the Kaiser's armies. Desperately short of munitions, the Russian artillery was subject to court martial if any gun fired more than three shells a day.

The British and French allies could not supply Russia through the Baltic, blocked by the German fleet, nor through the Dardanelles, closed by the Turks. The new trans-Siberian railway had a limited capacity, and Russia's traditional outlet to the Arctic oceans, the port of Archangel, was ice-locked for half the year.

Until the desperation of war, the Tsarist government had simply refused to take advantage of the Gulf Stream waters that keep this tiny corner of the Soviet arctic ice-free throughout the winter. 'Silly to plan a trading port on land that can feed only two cocks and three hens,' sniffed the distant regional governor.

But by 1915, Austrian prisoners of war and Chinese labourers were building the rail link to the new port.

During World War One, the allies shipped five million tons of supplies to the Tsar, about a million tons more than were shipped to Soviet Murmansk during World War Two. The port was also the base for the abortive British role in the war of intervention against the infant Bolshevik government.

They still tend the graves of Petty Officer Jack Case of HMS *Gossamer* and Merchant Seaman David Lamb of the SS *Empire Selwyn* and all the other RAF pilots, British and American seamen and gunners who died defending and supplying Murmansk against the German attacks by land, air and sea.

The Germans were based in Norway, less than 100 miles from Murmansk, which is still a battle zone of the secret war, with Nato electronic intelligence bases just across the border from the biggest concentration of military hardware in the Soviet Union.

The northern fleet is based there, 212 surface ships and 180 submarines, including 41 that can fire missiles, and almost 500 naval aircraft. Apart from escorting the nuclear submarines to their firing positions, their wartime task is to stop the convoys from the US that would keep Nato supplied in time of war. Their problem is to break out into the Atlantic, through the closely guarded narrow ocean channels between Greenland and Iceland, the Faroes and Scotland, into the killing grounds where the cargo ships must sail.

Thrusting out eastwards from the long fjord of Murmansk is the Kola Peninsula, with its airfields, radar networks and missile bases – the Russian version of East Anglia. The efficient Soviet statistical service gives the population of Murmansk alone as 420,000. Of these, 15,000 work in the fishing industry, and another 15,000 work in the merchant marine. Add in another 10,000 in the mines, and say 20,000 to run the city services, and the local officials are still at a loss to explain what the other 250,000 people of working age actually do.

'It is no secret that we have the base of the Northern Fleet near here,' Mr Alexander Dubrovin, the first secretary of the region said. 'Its task is purely defensive, to protect our homeland. We do not count the base in the economic life of the region, and do not even include it in our five-year plans. Our plans are based on the future, and the future we dream of is a nuclear-free arctic.'

Whatever the plans might say, the huge funds poured into Murmansk by the state since the explosive growth of the Soviet navy began – after the Cuba crisis – testify to the strategic importance of this little corner of Russia that the Gulf Stream warms.

The high salaries, and the glasshouse farms with their heavily subsidised electricity, and the neon lights and the prosperous shops, are all part of the price paid to support the fleet.

In their own way, the Russians acknowledge it. Murmansk is formally twinned with the American city of Jacksonville, the big US naval base, and the home port of the warships that will escort the Nato cargoes to their fateful rendezvous with the Murmansk submarine fleet.

Rural rides
3 August 1987

You could start a small war with the military equipment displayed on the road from Leningrad to Moscow. But you would have to prise the weaponry from the concrete first, because they are the set-pieces of war memorials.

On a recent drive, I counted one MiG-15 jet, still menacing in silver paint, a big 152 mm howitzer, one T-34 tank mounted on a sloping plinth, its barrel pointing at the sky, and even one of the early Katyushas, the truck-mounted rocket batteries that stunned Hitler's Wehrmacht when they first met them. An up-dated version is still in use today.

Ever since childhood, I have enjoyed those car journey games where you have to spot things, and the Moscow–Leningrad road is good for this because it remains so rural. Bear in mind that this is the main highway connecting the two greatest cities of the Soviet Union – 780 kilometres of prime motorway that in most other countries would be a teeming, six-lane concrete bore.

Not here. Outside Moscow and outside Leningrad, there are stretches of dual-carriageway, and on the by-pass around the big city of Kalinin and elsewhere there are long bits of lethal three-lane highway, where every attempt to overtake a lumbering lorry becomes a game of chicken.

And on the road to Moscow from Zavidovo, where Leonid Brezhnev kept a hunting lodge, there is even a Zil lane in the middle of the road, just like the ones in Moscow, where special tracks for VIPs are closed to ordinary traffic by two white lines.

But for long, long miles, this main artery of Soviet communications is a two-track country road, lumpy and pot-holed and lethal with the smears of damp hay or squashed vegetables that have fallen from the backs of ill-loaded trucks.

My other favourite car game is animal spotting, and on this last drive I counted three sets of sheep, two of cows, more chickens than I can recall and one flock of goats. Under my rules, you can only count the animals that actually cross the road in front of you. So livestock pottering in the gardens is not included. This was not a very memorable trip, because there was no pig dozing in the centre of the road to be steered around.

The other great spotting item is the village well. The sheer size of the Soviet Union and the cold of its winters makes a national piped water system an engineering project of mind-boggling proportions. So most of the villages along the road stick with the tried and tested technology of wells, and in places where modernity has invaded, a standpipe in the village street.

The wells are good for this game because you can subdivide them into ones with a communal bucket, ones with ropes or chains, painted ones or grotty ones. A prettily painted well is usually a good clue to the way the village feels about itself, whether the izbas, the traditional wooden cottages, will be kept in decent repair and painted, or whether the entire place assumes that rickety, collapsing, and generally rotting air that is a depressing feature of the Soviet countryside.

Another good sign is the old grannies sitting by the roadside, selling their garden produce from buckets. A bad village will have a token display of spuds, but you can stock up with sweet fat strawberries and new potatoes and fresh garlic and herbs still glistening from dew in a good village.

Vini is a good village, where the grannies firmly guard their buckets of strawberries from the interested sheep by waving sticks at them. The lakeside village of Edrovo, where we spotted the goats, was so picturesque that you would expect antique shoppes on every corner and over-priced restaurants and theme parks. Doubtless, all of these things will come as the family car and the leisure industry continue their inexorable transformation of Soviet life.

There were signs of it on the last two hours of the drive into Moscow early on a Friday evening, with the road from the city suddenly thickening into long queues as the dacha-owners headed out for the weekend at the country cottage.

We are watching a social revolution under way. There are two historical reasons for the decline of the Soviet village. One is the traditional dependence on the rail system for the bulk of national transport, and the other is the way the collective farm system has taken so many rural people from the izbas and decanted them into pre-fabricated concrete housing blocks.

But the private car and the dacha boom are changing all that, and the new opportunities for private enterprise will probably one day bring the roadside cafes and souvenir shops and sweep away the goats and pigs and the village wells. We shall just have to go back to spotting T-34 tanks at the war memorials as we speed along the Mos-Len Autoway, while turbo-charged Lada convertibles full of Soviet yuppies zoom past in the fast lane. The only question is how long it will take.

Bone idols

12 October 1987

Other peoples' faiths are always a tricky subject, but the curious kinds of religious mania currently taking place in the Soviet Union probably need the attentions of a social psychologist rather than a rather baffled news reporter. It seems to have begun with Chernobyl, a word which in the Ukrainian language can be translated as 'wormwood'.

Those familiar with Revelations, that book of the Bible which seems to have inspired a remarkable number of unusual sects, will recall that bit about a star falling from the sky for our sins, a star that will bring great plagues and foul rains falling and a terrible bitterness in the water.

The angel responsible for all this unpleasantness was called 'wormwood', and the effect of this coincidence upon the minds of more impressionable Ukrainians can be imagined.

We also have not one, but two millennial occasions looming ahead. Next year we shall celebrate the 1000th anniversary of the founding of Christianity in Russia, when the saintly Prince Vladimir of Kiev threw the pagan idols into the River Dnieper and established the Byzantine rites. The second is the year 2000, to which Mikhail Gorbachev often refers in his speeches, either as the target date for nuclear disarmament, or the goal to which his perestroika reform programme is working.

Ever since reading Norman Cohn's marvellous book *The Pursuit of the Millennium*, I have been aware that these anniversaries bring some curious things out of the woodwork.

In the case of the disused village church in the Ukraine village of Grushevo, it emerged from the balcony. A ten-year-old girl saw a woman's figure. Adults gathered, and within days, this emergence of the Virgin Mary was attracting the faithful from all across the Ukraine.

More sightings of the Virgin Mary followed, in Ternopol, Ozernaya, Berezhany and Kamenka-Bugskaya, to the confusion and alarm of party officials, who began by trying to impose fines on those who cried, 'I see her.' At the town of Kamenka-

Bugskaya, one militant atheist tried to put a stop to it all by throwing a brick through the window where she appeared.

All these were events of which I had read or heard, but had no personal experience. But on a visit to Kiev recently I took the opportunity to visit the Lavra, the monastic complex on the steep banks of the Dnieper that is one of the glories of the city. It is famous not only for the churches, but also for the catacombs where thousands of mummified corpses of priests and believers lie buried in the niches in the deep caves.

Since the monastery now works only as a museum, they are open to the public, and it is an eerie sight, the narrow white-walled tunnels with tiny side chapels filled with the long dead. Some niches contain simply heaps of skulls and bones, others a tidily-arranged single skeleton. The eminent priests and saints are usually wrapped in a white shroud, and their heads covered with a red purple cloth, embroidered with a skull and crossbones. Their mummified hands, brown and shrunken, peek from slits in the shroud.

I had recently read an article in *Ogonyak* magazine which said the mummies were falling into disrepair, and that the catacombs were in a shameful state. And indeed, there were some whose bones had broken through the skin, others whose fingers had crumbled and dropped away. Then we came upon a chapel slightly larger than the rest, containing twelve corpses in a neat row, under a single coverlet. Two old ladies, peasants from their dress, stood outside the chapel and preached to the visitors, who had to squeeze past them in the narrow tunnel.

'You must praise the Lord, and then your cares will disappear. You may lose love, or children or life, but praise the Lord and He will take you in His everlasting embrace,' they said. 'The Day of Judgement is at hand.' I stopped to listen, and asked them about the bodies in the chapel.

'It was a single family, twelve brothers, and they all died with straight limbs save the smallest,' she said. 'My grandmother brought me here, and told me that when that leg is straightened, it is the Lord's sign that the Day of Judgement is nigh,' she went on. 'And it is straight now,' broke in the other.

'The ungodly closed off this chapel to do repair work, and they straightened the leg. The Day of Judgement is coming to us. They have brought it on,' she said in great agitation.

They struck me as good, simple women. I know not the truth of all this, nor the strength of the legend of the twelve dead brothers and the bent leg, but I can confirm that there are curious things afoot down among the godly of the Ukraine. The angel wormwood, whom they call Chernobyl, has left a mark upon the land.